READY TO LAUNCH

Navigating the Transition from High School
to Post-Secondary Life –
A Guide for Ontario Students and Parents

Janet Hilliard

Copyright © 2022 by Janet Hilliard

All rights reserved

No part of this book may be reproduced, stored in a retrieval system, or transmitted by any means, electronic, mechanical, photocopying, recording, or otherwise, without written permission from the author or publisher. There is one exception. Brief passages may be quoted in articles or reviews.

Library and Archives Canada Cataloguing in Publication

CIP data on file with the National Library and Archives

ISBN 978-1-55483-513-3 for the trade paperback edition\
ISBN 978-1-55483-514-0 for the e-book edition

*To my children,
five unique individuals travelling
their own distinct life journeys.*

CONTENTS

Introduction	7
1. What You Need To Know About Launching	10
Time	11
Money	13
Effort	16
Motivation	18
Mindset	21
Readiness	24
Self-Regulation	24
Self-Efficacy	28
What Does it Mean to be Ready?	32
2. Who Are You?	34
Interests	36
Aptitudes	39
Strengths	42
Values	44
Where Might This Take You?	47
3. When You Don't Feel Ready	52
The Victory Lap	53
The Work World	55
Gap Year, Part 1	55
Heading to Work	56
Post-Secondary Preparatory Programs	57
General and Career Foundation Certificate programs	58
Academic Upgrading	59
Travel	60
Gap Year, Part 2	60
4. Where Does Your Future Lie?	62
Colleges	63
Universities	64
Military Careers and the Royal Military College of Canada	66
Private Colleges	67
Apprenticeships	68
Inter-Provincial and International Options	72

Distance Education – Online Learning	74
Narrowing Down Your Preferences	78
Personal Considerations – Your Needs	81
Program Considerations	83
Start Your Research	84
Alternate Pathways	85
Your Eligibility	87
Institution Considerations	90
First Impressions	91
Living Arrangements	92
Extracurriculars	93
Making Final Choices	94
5. How To Get There	**96**
University Applications	97
University Applicants Not Currently in Secondary School	100
University Offers of Admission	101
College Applications	102
College Applicants Not Currently in Secondary School	104
College Offers of Admission	105
Royal Military College Applications	105
Private College Applications	106
Inter-Provincial and International Applications	106
Not Accepted	107
Living Arrangements	109
Applying to Residence	109
Off-Campus Housing	111
Choosing a Roommate	113
Course Registrations	114
Paying for It	116
RESPs	116
Student Jobs	117
Scholarships and Bursaries/Grants	118
Bursaries	122
Government Subsidized Retraining Programs	123
Student Loans	123
Government Student Aid Programs	124
Bank and Private Loans	126
Tax Credits and Benefits	127

6. Launching	130
Academics	131
Food and Shelter	135
Finding Your People	137
Your Mental and Physical Health	139
Eating	142
Exercise	144
Sleep	146
Safety	149
Settling Into the New Normal	150
7. Changing Direction	152
What Next?	156
8. Your To Do List	159
Resources	162
Notes	170

INTRODUCTION

Finishing high school is a big accomplishment and a starting point for incredible change in a young adult's life. You may have already been asked many times what it is you're going to do next, where you're going to go, what you plan to do with your life.

There are two million Canadians studying in post-secondary institutions each year.[1] Perhaps you plan to join them!

As a student, you may be excited and apprehensive at the same time. You may have an image of college life gleaned from TV shows and movies, which is probably pretty inaccurate. You may be keen to be on your own, but a little worried about making new friends or keeping up with schoolwork or being able to pay your bills on time.

As a parent, you, too, may be both excited and apprehensive. Choosing a program and applying for post-secondary may be completely foreign to you. Perhaps you have never set foot in a college or university and have no idea how to go about the process or how to prepare your child for this transition. Or you may realize that things have changed a lot since you were in college or university – the number of options has quadrupled… as have the costs. You may have certain expectations for your child based on your own experiences, but remaining open-minded is essential. There's a pretty good chance that your child's journey will be different than yours.

The direct route from high school into post-secondary education is still the simplest and most straightforward for many students; however, both the rising cost and increasing number of specialized programs is making it more and more challenging for young students and their families. Students need to be able to make appropriate school and program choices, stay on top of their application and registration procedures, ensure they will be able to pay for everything, and be mature enough to follow through with their academic and personal responsibilities. This guide will lay out all the details for you.

That said, the direct route to post-secondary education is certainly not the only route to a satisfying career. Finishing high school can lead to change, growth and insight along many different paths, and it would be prudent to look at some of the alternate routes as well. The key is in having some ideas about what you would like to do in the future, finding out which directions hold the most potential for you personally, and making some plans for how to get there.

When should you start all this soul-searching and career preparation? Certainly not the week before you graduate, or the week after an application deadline! As early as grade nine, you can begin exploring careers through "Take Your Kid to Work" Day, adding to your scholarship potential through volunteerism, and building a school financing fund through part-time jobs. Ideally, you will start seriously considering your post-high school future by the time you're entering grade eleven. Starting in grade eleven will give you time to really analyze your goals and contemplate what kind of future appeals to you. It will also give you time to research all the pathways that get you there.

But what if you're already beyond high school? Post-secondary education is definitely not just for the young; it is no longer a milieu dominated by teens. The proportion of older adults undertaking college, university and apprenticeship programs has grown steadily, as the desire or the need to upgrade skills and qualifications – or to change careers completely – has gained acceptance within our increasingly changeable, global and technological economy. In fact, many post-secondary institutions are now focused on developing certificates and micro-credentials geared toward the very specific training needs of businesses and their employees.

You may be considered a "mature student" in the eyes of colleges if you are over 19 and don't have a high school diploma; universities, on the other hand, will consider you a "mature student" if you have been out of school and working for at least two years. In either case, if you are a mature student, you may have even more questions and deeper apprehension about starting a post-secondary program. You may have a family, a job and responsibilities – a more complicated existence than your younger classmates – but the information you find here will still be helpful in guiding you to consider your options and understanding the process required to reach your goal.

The purpose of this guide is to give you information to launch you into decisions about your future – your *near* future. The emphasis is on taking some first steps in the *direction* toward a satisfying career. You absolutely do not need to decide the rest of your life today, or this year, or even this decade! The future is wide open, as they say, and yet no one can really see it. No one can know without a doubt that this first *career direction* will be your last – in fact, believing that you've got your future all laid out is pretty limiting.

As Dr. Seuss said, "You have brains in your head. You have feet in your shoes. You can steer yourself any direction you choose."[2] All you need to do now is pick your *initial* direction and figure out how to start marching along it. You only need to plan your first step.

Think about yourself and what you want for your career at this moment, but keep your mind and your options open to ultimately enjoy a winding path through a long, satisfying life. This is just your launching point.

Please Note:
The term "parent" is used throughout this book; it is intended to also refer to any parental substitute, including legal guardians, foster parents, and other parental authorities.

1

WHAT YOU NEED TO KNOW ABOUT LAUNCHING
(First things first!)

When you were a kid, you probably had some definite plans for what you were going to be when you grew up. Fireman, princess, pop singer, hockey player, astronaut... You may have been told that you could be anything you want to be, and you may have believed that then, but now that you are actually in a position to choose a career direction it has become clear that some doors will be easier to open than others.

You may have known since you were five that you wanted to be a doctor, archaeologist, kindergarten teacher or industrial millwright, and if that dream still holds for you, great! If, on the other hand, you're not yet sure what you want to be when you grow up, have no fear. At this point, you are not required to pick a career for life; you are not even required to pick a career at all! All you need to figure out is one or two *potential career directions*: what will your first steps be on your journey toward a satisfying work life?

There are a few things to think about when figuring out what you're interested in and what potential career direction might work for you, since not all interesting careers are created equal. You want a career direction...

- that you would enjoy doing, to some degree
- that will earn you a decent income, whatever that means to you
- that will allow for a lifestyle that suits your preferences, such as travelling, or working from home, or having flexible hours, etc.

Most high school graduates go on to post-secondary education at some point, though they don't necessarily go right after high school, and they don't always stick with the first program they chose. But a certificate, diploma or degree will be a stepping-stone to a variety of possible paths in your future – a significant stepping-stone, and one with potential to take you in many different directions once you've earned it. You can't know where you'll actually end up until you get there.

Of course, no one can guarantee that it's going to be a smooth road. Your next steps involve more than just dreams; they also involve **time, money and effort**. And your likelihood of success as a post-secondary student is closely related to your **motivations** and your **mindset** along the way. Are you ready?

Time

Post-secondary studies are an investment in time: for most students, this means time spent studying instead of earning a full-time income, time spent doing homework instead of having fun, and perhaps time spent away from home instead of with family.

The amount of time spent in your post-secondary education can vary widely, from less than one year earning a college certificate in aircraft structural repair or personal support work, for example, to ten years or more to become a doctor or professor. In the past, it was generally expected that the longer one spent in post-secondary studies, the better one's income and working conditions would be in the end. This does not always ring true anymore. Most graduates with that one-year Aviation Structural Engineering certificate will have more opportunities and earn more one year after graduating than a graduate with a 4-year degree in psychology, hospitality or fine art. That's not to say that those 4-year degrees are in any way less valuable; they simply have outcomes that run along a different timeline. Understanding the length of time it will take to achieve the kind of career you want is an important consideration.

How much time are you willing to spend on your education?

Investing time in post-secondary studies is still known to be the best way to achieve a full-time career that pays more than minimum wage. In fact, Canadian statistics show that college graduates earn about twice as much as high school graduates and, over the course of twenty years of work, those with a university bachelor's degree will earn from $448,000 (for women) to $732,000 (for men) more than those with only a high school diploma.³ The time it takes to reach graduation can often be flexible, with part-time alternatives, optional work placement program extensions, and program-integrated co-op options. This kind of information is not always easy to find, so if time may be an issue for you, it would probably be worthwhile to talk to a program coordinator or admissions expert at your potential post-secondary institution(s) to see how their program might accommodate your timeline preferences.

[margin note: You may have options]

If you are unencumbered by time restraints and looking for deeper learning options, choosing a program with an internship or co-op option is likely to give you valuable work experiences that will greatly enhance your future employability options, taking longer to complete but often earning you a decent wage along the way. Of course, some students may eventually choose to extend their learning time *after* graduation, either by choosing a different direction or by delving deeper into their chosen topic by taking a Masters or PhD program.

Think of your time investment on a smaller scale as well. The amount of time you're willing or able to spend on your education *each week* will determine how long it will take to complete your program, and how well you will do in each course. Each of your classes might require only a few hours of your time each week, but for each one of those classes you may expect to spend an additional two to ten hours per week studying, learning in labs or clinics, completing homework, etc. The time invested in your future can be measured week by week and day by day.

Bear in mind that, within the first one or two years of post-secondary education, scores of students find that they are not happy with their initial choice of program or institution. Anywhere from 15 to 50% are likely to withdraw, depending on the program.⁴ For many, this means switching to a different program, sometimes starting over and extending the overall time spent in reaching their goal of graduation. In fact, changing programs or changing schools seems to be the new norm in the current post-secondary state of increasingly specific and streamed programs that may surprise and overwhelm new students. Hopefully, this guide will help reduce your likelihood of time spent in indecision and discontent! Do not be afraid to make changes, however – remember that life is a long and winding road and you're only just beginning your journey.

Questions to ask yourself:

- How much time are you willing and able to spend to get to a career that you find satisfying?
- How much time will it take to reach the career(s) that you're considering?
- Are there options for part-time or flexible learning in a program you're considering?
- Are there options to take your learning further if you wish, earning extra qualifications, graduate certificates, or a graduate or professional degree?
- "Time is money." Do your finances align with the cost of a potentially lengthy education?

Money

Post-secondary education is not cheap!

Being able to pay for tuition and living costs while in post-secondary education is a huge issue for many, many students. The cost of delivering programs has steadily increased over the past two decades, largely due to the growth in expensive technologies and the constant need to upgrade equipment for learning. At the same time, government subsidization of these costs has been declining, leaving students to foot the increasingly heavy bill.

Tuition fees for college and university programs vary widely. *Tuition fees* The average cost of one year's tuition for diploma programs at Ontario's colleges runs from about $2400 to $6100, depending on the type of program;[5] for a university undergraduate degree program, the average was $8899/year in 2020.[6] Specialized or

Other fees very technical programs, such as engineering or heavy equipment operation, cost even more. Supplementary fees, as well as any required textbooks and equipment, are an additional expense, often to the tune of hundreds or even thousands of dollars, depending on the program. Some programs, like dental hygiene, graphic arts or vehicle maintenance, may have very high initial costs for required tools or technology that students must purchase before starting the program.

Cost of housing The cost of living will also vary depending on your accommodations and the location of your school. Living at home is generally the cheapest way to go, although there are likely some program limitations and experiential drawbacks to this option. If you will be moving away from home, living in residence is usually a more expensive choice, but it offers stability and safety in your new environment, and is usually a practical option that provides not only a convenient living space but a meal plan and an abundant social scene without having to pay for a full year's lease. Choosing to rent a room, an apartment, or a whole house with a group of friends provides more independence, but you will need to consider the cost of a lease, food preparation, transportation to school and grocery stores, etc. Many college and university student associations maintain off-campus housing portals with local information and listings. Be sure to research the housing options and average costs for any institution you're considering. You can read more about this in Chapters 5 and 6.

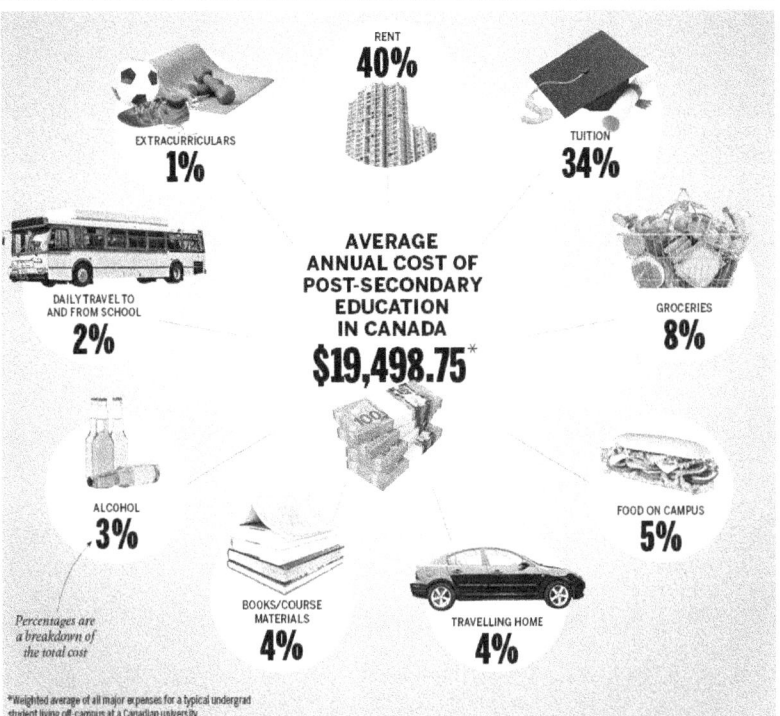

Image from "The cost of a Canadian university education in six charts," by M. Brown, 2018, Macleans. https://www.macleans.ca/education/the-cost-of-a-canadian-university-education-in-six-charts/

So, all told, you may be shelling out anywhere from $3000 to over $20,000 per year for your education, depending on what you take and where you take it. And yet, a post-secondary education is a financial investment that can produce an exceptionally great return in so many ways! Aside from improving the likelihood of finding satisfying work that meets your interests and needs, completing a post-secondary education provides a significant increase in your future income. Data from the 2016 census tells the story:

In 2021, the average yearly income of Ontarians who had...
A high school diploma $51,930
A college diploma $60,896 (even higher with trades certificates)
A university bachelor's degree $83,597

"Average Annual Employment Income by Educational Attainment and Age Group, 2016 Census. Statistics Canada, Catalogue no. 98-400-X2016253. https://ontariosuniversities.ca/wp-content/uploads/2021/02/Table-5-Average-Annual-Employment-Income-by-Educational-Attainment-and-Age-Group.pdf

How will you find the money for this fantastic investment opportunity? Sources of funding, including Registered Education Savings Plans, student jobs, scholarships and grants/bursaries, government subsidized retraining programs, and government and private student loans, will all be covered in some detail in the "Paying for It" section of Chapter 5. The option of a paid education is also offered by the Canadian Armed Forces – read about that in Chapter 4.

Questions to ask yourself:

- Approximately how much money will you need each year for program tuition and fees, books, equipment, rent, food, transportation, entertainment, etc.?
- Do you have a source of funds that will cover your post-secondary expenses?
- Do you plan to work while at school? Part-time, or full-time?
- Is having your education paid for by the Canadian Armed Forces something you might consider?

Effort

Was high school easy for you, or did you struggle to understand new concepts or get your homework done? In many ways, post-secondary courses are very similar to those in high school, except that you will probably not have teachers pushing you to keep up. You will be completely responsible for following through and living with the consequences, good or bad. There are many supports available that provide assistance, but it will be up to you to seek out help if you need it. Ultimately, how much effort you are willing to put into your education will determine your level of success.

For most people, post-secondary schooling requires plenty of effort. In order to do well, you will need to be organized, be on time for all your classes, exercise self-discipline to study and complete all your assigned work, use your willpower to make sure you get enough sleep, eat healthy food and get plenty of exercise. Are you prepared to put in the necessary effort? Some students think it's going to be easy and then are surprised to find themselves missing classes or homework; other students are afraid that they're not ready and won't be able to handle it and are surprised to discover that they had it in them all along.

The amount of effort you put into your post-secondary studies boils down to your habits. If you already have strong study habits, you're ahead of the game. The majority of new post-secondary students share one very common habit that can become overwhelming, causing anxiety, failure and self-loathing: procrastination.

Get a handle on your procrastination habits now! Take note of when you tend to procrastinate with schoolwork; what is the cue that makes you avoid doing it? Difficulty, disinterest, tiredness, hunger, other responsibilities…? What is it that you do instead? Take charge of cues that cause you to avoid working by thinking logically about the benefits of doing the work and the consequences of not doing the work. Prioritize the items that are most important, and instead of just *planning* to get them done, actually *schedule* a time to do them.

Procrastination cues and distractions

When you do get down to work, what are the distractions that are most likely to steal your focus away? Figure out how to control them. For example, find a quiet spot to work; prepare your workspace so you have everything you need at hand; use computer access blockers, study apps and focus timers; disable your phone notifications; set a timer for half an hour of focus time; and make it clear to others that you don't want to be disturbed.

Often, the most difficult part of procrastination to defeat is the "getting started" part. If it's hard to start studying or working on an assignment, it could be that the job is too big. Break it down into smaller parts, and choose to spend only half an hour working on one small first step, like starting to write down some ideas for an essay, or writing just the introduction for a lab report. If studying for an exam seems daunting, spend only half an hour looking through the items to be reviewed and deciding which ones are most important to practice and which ones you already understand. If the topic of a report is uninteresting to you, spend just half an hour searching the library website for potential resources. Getting started is the most common procrastination issue; committing to just one short half hour of effort will get you started, then you can reward yourself with something more interesting, like a game, a snack, a chat with a friend, or a walk in the sunshine. Make thirty minutes your standard focus period – half an hour of effort is usually doable, and further short half hours of effort will eventually get you to the finish line.

Fortunately, it is really not so difficult to develop new, better habits. It does take time and some practice, though, so get started right away. And your ability to maintain those good habits for post-secondary success depends largely on your **motivation** and your **mindset**. You need to want it, and you need to know that you can do it.

Questions to ask yourself:

- How much effort have you put into your learning in the past? Will you need to improve your level of effort to achieve your post-secondary goals?

- Is procrastination a common problem for you? If so, what are your procrastination cues and distractions?

- Do you believe you can change your habits, if necessary? Are you willing to try?

Motivation

Why do you do what you do? Why are you doing this? What is your motivation? (Or *who* is your motivation?)

Internal vs. external motivators

Motivation comes in two forms: external and internal. *External* motivators are things or people or circumstances that can affect the choices you make. They are usually things over which you have very little control, like your cultural traditions, your parents' or teachers' opinions, or your financial situation. In contrast, you do have control over the *internal* motivators, like your personal values, attitudes, beliefs and desires that inspire your purpose and goals.

EXAMPLES OF EXTERNAL MOTIVATORS	EXAMPLES OF INTERNAL MOTIVATORS
Cultural traditions or expectations regarding certain careers	Personal interests and values, like helping others, building things, discovering or leading
Systemic barriers to certain careers	Ambition
Parents' opinions or level of support	Curiosity and imagination
Financial struggles	Thirst for knowledge
Family obligations	Seeking financial stability

If you have the freedom, the competence and the means to make choices based solely on your own internal motivations – to be whatever you want to be – you are very fortunate! All you need to do is to figure out which path you want to choose and commit to working toward your goals. You may not yet feel confident in making choices or establishing a goal, but at least you have the liberty to take the next steps once you are ready.

External motivators may either subconsciously or very deliberately encourage you to take a path that may not be what you, yourself, are internally motivated to pursue. For example, where you live, your culture or your economic status can be external motivators that affect the choices you *want* to make or *are able to* make, and sometimes these external motivators can't be avoided. The problem is that when we make decisions based on external motivations, we are much less likely to be successful and happy in the end. As you develop your plans, think carefully about *what* career choices you make and *why* you make them. What are your motivations?

If your motivation to take a certain program or strive for a specific career is external (say, your parents or your community), are you afraid that choosing a different path will dis-

Think about the effect of external motivators

appoint them? Perhaps this would be a good time to have a discussion with them about your wishes and their influence on your decisions, to clear the air and get everyone on the same page. Open communication is, after all, the fastest route to understanding. Or, if difficult external motivators are really holding you back, perhaps getting help and considering ways to compromise or to change your circumstances can reduce their impact. Talking through problems like this with an academic or career counsellor in a high school, post-secondary institution, government employment or social services office, or in a private counselling office, may be extremely beneficial.

Parents' Note:
You are likely a significant external motivator for your child. As your child starts developing a post-secondary plan, consider the ways in which you might be affecting the choices they make. What are your expectations for your child? How much influence do you have on their educational decisions and career direction? Do you assume your child will go directly to a university because that's what you did, for instance, or are you open to learning more and accepting other post-secondary options? Have you alluded that you think you know what decisions would be best for them? Are you willing to explore the benefits of a gap year, so your child can work, travel, and have other new learning experiences? Understanding all of your child's options, pointing out any potential roadblocks, and offering thoughtful, unbiased advice will help you support your child in making well-informed and appropriate decisions that are right for them.

Action can create motivation!

People often believe that they are less likely to do a good job at a task that they're not very motivated to do. This is a common (and poor) excuse used by students to explain their lack of action. In fact, you do not need to feel motivated to do a task in order to actually do it. Motivation isn't required to create action; action can actually create motivation! Forcing yourself to take just one small step – to begin an assignment, start filling out an application or make a little change in the way you do things – is often all it takes to get you moving. Once you're on your way, taking more small steps becomes easier; you've found the energy, the motivation, to keep going. In other words, if you just *do something*, you can "fake it 'til you make it."[7]

Questions to ask yourself:

- Why do you tend to do the things you do, in general?
- Are your motivations internal or external, or both? What – or who – is motivating you?
- Do you feel you will be able to make decisions about your future with unconditional support from the people who are important to you?
- Who can you talk to about external motivators that may negatively affect your choices and create barriers to your success?
- Are you in the habit of starting things, even though you may not feel particularly motivated? Do you have the capacity to just do it?

Mindset

What's your attitude? Do you feel at least somewhat capable of succeeding? Do you believe you can learn, even though you might need help sometimes? Are you afraid of failure because you think it will reflect on your value as a person?

Everyone can learn. How you *feel* about the work of learning largely determines what and how well you will learn.

Having a **fixed mindset** means you believe your intelligence and your learning capacity are static and unchanging. If you have a fixed mindset, you may think that your brain can only hold so much information, or that you'll never be able to understand math/French/spelling/chemistry, and that being unable to solve a problem right away reflects badly on your intelligence. Failure is frightening and makes you feel stupid. Those who have a fixed mindset tend to exhibit a more pessimistic outlook and are less likely to achieve their goals because they're not so good at dealing positively with challenges... and there definitely will be challenges along the way!

In research by Dr. Carol Dweck, a psychologist who first noted the connection between mindset and learning, students with a fixed mindset defined themselves as failures when they experienced academic difficulties. "And the more depressed they felt, the more they let things go; the less they took action to solve their problems. For example, they didn't study when they needed to, they didn't hand in their assignments on time, and they didn't keep up with their chores."[8] These students did not believe in their own ability to learn and succeed through hard work and focus.

If you have a **growth mindset**, on the other hand, you don't feel the need to prove your intelligence. You believe that you are capable of learning – you have potential – even if you will need assistance or a different schedule or changes to your environment to do so. You know that learning often requires hard work, but the hard work will result in the growth of skills and intelligence. In fact, no amount of talent will bring you success *without* hard work – just ask Elon Musk, Stephen King, Kevin Durant or Paul McCartney!

To those with a growth mindset, failure is understood to be a result of lack of experience and skill, which can be changed. Students with a growth mindset aim to develop their intelligence and abilities, and view problems and challenges as opportunities to stretch themselves and learn from their mistakes. Clearly, students who have a growth mindset will have an easier time taking on any challenges and are more likely to be successful in their educational journey and in achieving their goals.

Parents' Note:
You can encourage the development of a growth mindset in your child. When they are experiencing difficulty with schoolwork or with relationships, remind them that their learning is a process. They may not feel capable yet, they may not have the answers yet, but they are learning and growing from their experiences. Hard work does eventually lead to accomplishments of all sorts, so acknowledge and praise the effort your child expends, even if it doesn't always result in the desired success. It's okay if they're not there just yet – they may get there eventually!

So a growth mindset is like positive thinking. It frees you to persevere through and even *welcome* challenges, take risks, and learn from your mistakes along the way.

Many students start this new chapter in their lives with a completely positive outlook, looking forward to the fun social scene and the fascinating topics of learning (but mostly the fun social scene), and by midterms realize that it's more work than fun and more routine than fascinating. Frankly, it's just life, with its typical "good, bad and ugly." Can you think positively about the good, *and* the bad… and even the ugly?

Note that having a growth mindset embraces the understanding that no one goes through life alone, and no one is expected to have all the answers, particularly when transitioning to a new situation. Getting help is just part of the process. You can absolutely *expect* to need help figuring out what to do, how and where to do it, and even whom you need to ask for help in the first place! There are so many knowledgeable and helpful people in the post-secondary community who can offer you not only the answers to your questions, but also lessons and inspiration for your own journey. Those resource people will be mentioned throughout this book – use them!

Questions to ask yourself:

- What's your attitude? Do you feel that you generally have a fixed mindset or a growth mindset when it comes to learning?
- Are you afraid of failure? Do you ever doubt that success is a possibility for you?
- Do you feel capable of succeeding, even if you're not there yet? Do you look forward to challenging tasks and believe you can learn, even though you might need help sometimes?
- Do you accept that you will almost certainly need help in order to navigate your new circumstances and be successful in your new learning? Are you willing to ask for help when you need it?

"Readiness"

Another important thing to understand about yourself is your level of readiness for undertaking a post-secondary program. Do you possess the good sense and independence it will take to achieve your academic goals? In order to be a successful student, you must be capable of self-regulation and have some self-efficacy.

Self-regulation

Self-regulation is when you have enough maturity, understanding and self-discipline to make positive, effective choices. It's being sensible, conscientious and responsible. When it comes to post-secondary education, there are choices to be made on a daily basis.

If you will be attending an institution away from your family, the comforts of home and the familiarity of your hometown, your first few months may prove to be a struggle as you adapt to a level of self-regulation that you have probably not needed in the past. You will likely have to learn to manage your eating, sleeping, studying, exercising, partying, shopping... So many new aspects of your life to control when you're on your own for the first time can feel exciting at first, then overwhelming a month or so later, when the honeymoon is over and daily life becomes routine, laundry piles up, grades start to come in, and you really crave a home-cooked meal. The vast majority of first-year students who are on their own for the first time will experience this. Fortunately, the changes themselves bring about both academic and personal growth that increase self-regulation, and, with some assistance, most students will settle in before too long.

Once again, *support* is key in developing self-regulatory habits. You have had influential adults helping you to develop self-regulatory skills since you were small, teaching you things such as which foods are more nutritious than others and how to prepare them, how to dress appropriately for the weather, how to ride a bicycle or take a bus or drive a car to get somewhere, how to use the washer and dryer... and, hopefully, allowing you to make mistakes and learn from the consequences.

Parents' Note:
Have you been helping your child develop the self-regulatory skills they'll need to be successful post-secondary students? Can your child complete homework without being nagged? Do they know how to do some basic cooking and use the laundry machines? Are they likely to feed themselves and get enough sleep if you're not around? Have they ever taken a bus or a train, or bought groceries? Can they create a budget and manage their finances? If not, today is the perfect day to get started on this "life" education!

Post-secondary students may get self-regulation support from professors who send reminders about upcoming deadlines, classmates who form study groups, or residence advisors who check in on them. Students with special needs will be able to access learning accommodations in their post-secondary institution. Many students find further support from the school's counselling or student services specialists, who offer training on self-management skills. And, naturally, with so many academic choices to be made every day, students will still have

Learning self-regulation skills

many opportunities to learn from their mistakes!

You will make academic choices that show your level of self-regulation every day, starting with the level of effort you put into your schoolwork – that level of effort discussed previously. For example, if you have pages to read in a textbook or an online resource, you could…

1. Choose to not do any of it
2. Choose to do some of the reading – make it feel like or look like you're doing something
3. Choose to do all the reading
4. Choose to do all the reading, and take some notes on the material that's new to you or that you might have to remember for an assignment or test
5. Choose to do all the reading, take notes, quiz yourself on the material, and then review the notes and quiz yourself again a couple days later

Which of these choices is going to reap the greatest academic reward? Is giving a semi-effective effort going to get you where you want to be? You can choose to act in any way you like, but not all these choices show enough self-regulation to lead you to the success that you probably seek.

In addition to the level of effort put into their studies, successful students turn their self-regulatory choices into positive *habits*. As you know, habits are behaviour patterns that become ingrained, like always putting your keys in a specific spot when you come home, or always having a cup of coffee when you wake up in the morning, or always watching an online lecture when it becomes available instead of leaving it until the day the homework is due. Habits develop from repeating our behaviour choices and, as mentioned earlier, they can be changed!

Of course, there are a number of self-regulating behaviours that are well known to increase academic success. You probably already know what they are, but do you *do* them? Actually *making these choices* and allowing them to become habits will jump-start a truly positive academic journey. The most productive choices for students include:

Turning choices into habits

- Setting goals and planning all the steps needed to achieve them
- Focusing and actively listening in on-campus and online classes
- Taking notes on lectures and readings, and keeping these notes and other resources organized
- Reviewing notes regularly and preparing well in advance for tests
- Working with a classmate or getting a tutor when having difficulty with content
- Making focusing easier by completing required work, being prepared with all necessary materials, sitting close to the instructor, finding a quiet study space, and – most importantly – turning off distractions like cellphones
- Planning your time to keep on top of your class schedule, due dates and deadlines
- Self-consequating – creating consequences for your own behaviours, such as allowing yourself the reward of playing a video game after completing homework

All of that said, making less effective choices one day, or for a week or even for years, does not mean that you cannot transform your habits — you can definitely start making better choices today. After all, this new post-secondary experience might be one of the biggest changes in your life so far, and you will be learning as much about yourself as you will about pipefitting, chemistry, linguistics or avionics. If necessary, will you have the self-regulatory ability to allow yourself to learn from your mistakes, start fresh and make new choices?

Questions to ask yourself:

- Do you feel mature enough to live on your own and do what's necessary to be successful, or at least to give it a try and expect to learn from your mistakes?
- Are you prepared to work hard in all your classes? Do you agree that effort and focus are more important than ability or talent?
- Are you willing to put away your electronic devices and other

distractions when you need to focus on your work?
- Are you willing and able to seek out and accept help if things aren't going well?

Self-efficacy

Efficacy means being able to take care of things; being *effective* in producing a result. *Self*-efficacy is about autonomy and self-reliance – being able to take care of yourself, and being effective in getting results (or information or help) when you need them. And it's very empowering.

You may have strong self-regulatory behaviours that help you to earn the good marks you want. However, if you end up having to pay late fees because you didn't know when your tuition was due, or you fail an exam because you were too afraid to ask about an academic accommodation that you need, or you can't graduate because you didn't know you had to take two social sciences electives, or you just generally feel awkward about asking for help… then self-efficacy is something you need to work on.

As the poet John Donne said, no man is an island. You are not alone. You are not alone in your situation as a student with crucial classes, possibly with a job, possibly with kids, possibly with terrible internet and twenty bucks in the bank and some confusion and stress and lots of questions.

Fortunately, no one expects a new student to have all the answers. Post-secondary institutions all have helpful resources for you to access both online and on-campus. All you need to do is *ask*.

There are people who want to help you learn and be successful – not only because that's their job, but because they actually take pleasure in your success. But they won't know you need help until you communicate that. So, all you require is to be able to communicate: get what you need, when you need it. And once you've found the answers or learned about the process one time, you will be better prepared to do this on your own next semester, building your independence, self-confidence and self-efficacy. You will have learned how to help yourself.

Getting what you need, when you need it!

As a capable, independent adult student, how will you know when to seek out help? How much time can you be expected to spend searching for answers on often unwieldy institutional websites and video tutorials? The same rule of thumb will work for you as a student as it works for employees in the work world.

The 15-Minute Rule
"According to the 15-Minute Rule, when an employee gets stuck on a problem, they have to adopt the mindset of a solution-finder and hammer away at it for 15 more minutes before they can ask for help.During this time period, they have to document everything they did that didn't work, so that they can give context to the person helping them.
Finally, once the 15 minutes are up, they must ask for help.This rule helps the employee strike a balance: they learn to be independent and figure things out for themselves, but they don't waste a ton of time if they're truly stuck.Adopting this rule as a student can prove very useful. You'll spend some time looking for your own answers and solve a lot of problems independently that you'd originally ask for help on. And when you do ask for help, you show that you take the problem seriously and that you're not just crying out for help the moment things get tough."[9]

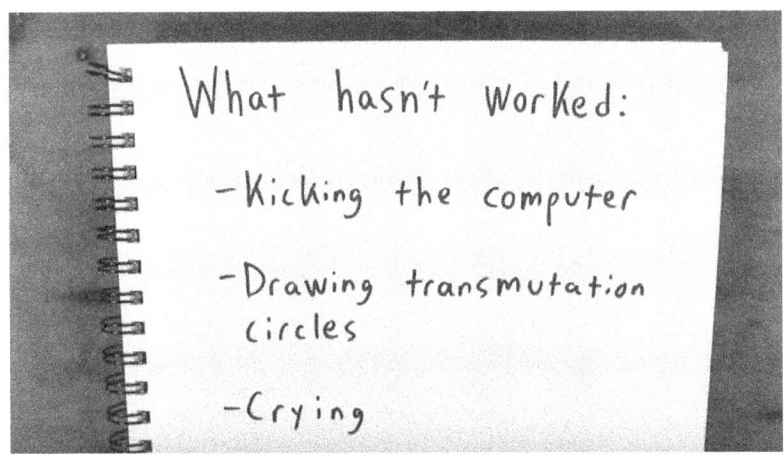

How to get answers to your questions

When you've tried but haven't been able to figure out the answer to your problem, whom can you ask? Who will have the information you need? If you need help with the content from one of your classes, your first source will be your own notes, textbook, or any recorded lectures. Joining a chat group or study group with your classmates is often a great route to get questions answered (though reliability won't be guaranteed). Course instructors, teaching assistants and lab instructors are generally available to answer questions via email, or through in-person or virtual office hours. If you need information about registering for courses, paying fees, changing programs, athletics, tutors, or any other academic, career, physical or mental health supports, you may have to step a little further to get what you need.

Specific information can often be received simply by emailing an address on the school's website. In many cases, though, particularly in larger institutions, email communications are slow and may even lead to further questions. Unfortunately, many young students are accustomed to A) communicating mainly through messaging apps, and/or B) having their parents keep track of their calendar, finances, transportation, etc. Asking for help may feel awkward and even intimidating. Having to make a phone call or speak to someone in person can cause anxiety if a student hasn't already had opportunities to practice with some support in less significant situations. Yet, the immediacy of phone or in-person contact very often leads to the quickest and most accurate result.

Parents' Note:
Parents are often used to doing everything for their child, because it's quicker and easier that way. In order to build your child's self-efficacy, give them opportunities to handle their own affairs. Whenever possible, have them call to make their own appointments, make their own arrangements for transportation, or deal with minor problems on their own. Give them support by discussing how best to go about these tasks, and offer encouragement when they are successful (or if they're not). Your child will be better prepared to take care of things independently and will be more likely to get what they need as soon as they need it in the future.

If getting phone or in-person help is difficult for you (as it is for many people), *prepare in advance*.

1. Look online to figure out where you might be able to get the information you need, for example an admissions, registrar, advising, counselling, student success, faculty/program or career development office. Chances are, even if you contact the wrong place, you will be redirected to the correct one. Find out where this office is and even who works there, if you can. Write down the phone number, location, etc. *Prepare yourself to get help!*
2. Think about exactly what you want to say, and practice it. Write it down in note form or even full sentences. Include every question or scenario you wonder about, so nothing gets missed and you can get a clear picture with all your questions answered at once. Having speaking notes is often appreciated by the person you meet with, since there is less likelihood of confusion or miscommunication. And, if you're speaking over the phone or leaving a voicemail, no one will even know that you're reading your notes.
3. Be prepared to write down the information you're given. You can't expect to remember any dates, addresses, phone numbers, names, course numbers, websites, or anything else mentioned. Writing them down also shows that you're taking responsibility for following through.
4. Follow through. You know what you need to do next, so don't put it off and possibly forget about it – do it asap!
5. Buy yourself a smoothie for having gotten what you needed when you needed it and proven your self-efficacy.

Developing the ability and *willingness* to communicate early on will lead to a great level of self-efficacy in a responsible, independent adult student – one of the most beneficial soft skills for anyone to have.

Questions to ask yourself:

- Do you have all the information you need? If not, do you know how to find it?

- Do you have an effective system to keep track of due dates and deadlines, not only for class activities but for fees, registrations, withdrawals, extracurriculars, etc.?
- Are you willing and able to communicate and seek help, to get what you need as soon as you need it?

What Does it Mean to be Ready?

There has been a great deal said so far about knowing yourself, figuring out what you want, and being mature and confident enough to take your next big step toward independent adulthood. Maybe now you're feeling a lot of pressure to make important decisions, and feeling even less ready to do so. Maybe you have doubts. Maybe "adulthood" is just too much to ask for. Maybe you're not sure if you're *emotionally ready*.

Emotional readiness Yes, emotional readiness is a pretty important factor in achieving success on your journey. But emotional readiness – as in maturity and self-management – comes with time and new experiences.

This is not the movies, where you do some soul searching, make an undeniably wise decision, and move smoothly into the next scene. No one expects you to suddenly experience some flash of insight or self-understanding that leads you to an inner well of maturity, confidence and determination that you didn't even know you had. Sure, you might surprise yourself! But, more likely, you will need some time and new experiences to reach the level of maturity and confidence that makes you feel *really ready*... and by then, you'll already be halfway to the future.

So, if you are currently in high school, please know that you are exactly as your future teachers, advisors, employers and friends expect you to be. You are expected to be inexperienced and unsure of yourself. You're expected to make mistakes and change plans. You are *not* expected to know how to feel or what to do in all the situations you will encounter. You are *not* expected to have decided on a clear path for your life. You are certainly *not* expected to move on without help and support.

Emotional readiness comes with doing something you *want* to do. We are all much more likely to do what it takes to succeed when we are personally invested in a goal.

High school comes to an end. You can't stay there forever – they do boot you out eventually. So you are forced to move on, and what you feel ready to move on *to* is all that is in question here.

You need a desire to *do* something – something chosen by you, not by anyone else. If you *want* to go into an apprenticeship program and you meet the eligibility requirements, there's a pretty good chance you're *ready* to do so. If you *want* to get a job, or to take a program in college or university, you're probably ready. Having the desire and planning the path to success is half the battle! And if you pursue a path that isn't really what you want, you may find out soon enough that you weren't ready for *that*.

Readiness may not be as complicated as you think.

Parents' Note:
Do you feel your child is ready for the challenges of post-secondary education? Are you ready for your child's next steps? Sometimes parents mistakenly consider their child unready to move on, when, in actuality, it is their own unwillingness to let their child go that is holding the child back. The transition from the stable routines of high school and family life to the independence of adulthood may be harder on the parent than the child. Again, think carefully about how you influence your child's next steps, and let your child be the judge of their readiness.

Questions to ask yourself:

- Were you able to answer most of the previous "Questions to Ask Yourself" at least somewhat positively?

- Even if you're feeling kind of nervous or anxious (which is normal), do you feel at least somewhat prepared to face the challenges of post-secondary education?

2.

WHO ARE YOU?
(What do you want to be when you grow up?)

In the previous century, having a good career was about finding a reliable job that you wouldn't mind doing every day, and that would give you enough money to pay the bills and enjoy a decent lifestyle. In this century, the career focus has shifted to "finding your passion," a catchphrase encouraging some kind of work that makes you feel fulfilled and energized because you simply love doing it.

You may have actually been asked, either jokingly or in all seriousness, "what is your passion?" We're told that we need to discover our passions in order to build a career around them and ensure our future satisfaction. It's a pressure-filled question that can be intimidating for many people, especially young adults with little life experience.

In fact, many people really don't know what their "passion" is or doubt that they will ever actually have one, so they end up:

a   Choosing a first path of interest and taking many detours toward other interests along the way
b   Waiting for inspiration/luck/desperation to hit, then picking whatever promising option will work
c   Never actually feeling passionate about anything in particular, but somehow ending up with a satisfying and happy life anyway

So, when asked "what's your passion," do you have an answer? Most people don't, but if *you* do, then great! You will probably want to follow it. But before jumping headlong into one single trajectory, do your homework and make sure you'll be happy with *all* the aspects of this potentially passion-charting career. For example, how much time and effort are you willing to put in to reach your goal? If your passion is in the creative arts – fine art or practical art or acting or writing or filmmaking – are you willing to live with less and persist in marketing yourself and dealing with rejection for whatever length of time it takes to become established – possibly decades? Are you prepared to put in an often-overwhelming amount of work, if your dream is to start your own business? This also goes for the sciences, which can require decades of education and experience if you want to become an expert in your field or do life-changing research.

Some passions may also not financially sustain your desired lifestyle. For example, if you really love oil painting, but also want a family, a big house and a nice car, you might look for compatible careers that will use your talents and passion for art but are more stable or more lucrative. Other passions may anticipate working conditions that don't suit your personality. If you absolutely love math and statistics but don't like spending most of your time working on your own or at a computer, you might consider enjoying math in a more varied career that involves working with others, such as doing scientific studies or teaching.

Investigate & analyze your passions

In some cases, a passion may not be your best choice for a career, but passions often make excellent hobbies. Perhaps you'd be happier enjoying your passion as a leisure pursuit or as a side gig while choosing a different line of work to pay the bills. Finding a balance with a career that both provides some enjoyment and also sustains you financially is an excellent goal.

Balance is essential

Most students can't identify an actual *passion*, but this doesn't mean they won't be able to start moving toward an interesting and valuable career. Most people do have a variety of *interests*, though not a specific one they'd really describe as a passion. A better question, then, might simply be "what are your interests?"

Interests

Who determines what your interests are? You do. Not your parents, your friends, your teachers or anyone else. As you know, other people who influence your career choices are external motivators, who may unintentionally encourage you to take a path that may or may not be what you, yourself, are inspired to pursue. The best way to succeed in anything is to do the things that you are internally motivated to do – the things that actually *interest* you. You will find greater satisfaction in work that has qualities matched to your interests.

Your interests are the things you like to learn about, and don't mind practicing. They are also the *environment* that you prefer to be in, such as a social environment with lots of friends, or quiet solitude, or being outside surrounded by nature.

Research any careers related to each interest

So if you have an interest in a certain area, explore it. Do some research. What career directions could it lead you toward? What kind of work might you end up doing? Find out everything you can about any career that seems to match your interests – you'll find some questions to guide your research in the "What Are You Aiming For?" section at the end of this chapter.

You may have a secret interest in something you've never tried before, and maybe you feel a bit nervous about saying it publicly if it's unusual or if you've had no prior experience with it. Don't let your fear stop you – prepare for any questions by doing plenty of research, then reach out for support from a family member, friend, guidance counsellor or mentor.

What if you've got *lots* of interests and need to narrow them down to make choices for your next steps? Or what if you're having a hard time coming up with any particular interests at all?

There are many interest inventories you can do online that may or may not be helpful in clarifying and putting into words the kinds of interests that you lean toward. For the most part, these tests are more like self-surveys, where you simply indicate whether you like or dislike each of the activities listed. This can pose a problem with accuracy, though, since very often they include activities you may never have actually experienced, such as baking, fixing cars, or wiring a computer. How can you know if you like them or not?

Even without completing a test, you can make a list of activities you like to do or working conditions that would interest you. Some examples:

Things I'm interested in doing	Work environment that I would prefer
Building things	Working outside
Drawing	Lots of interaction with co-workers
Manipulating numbers	Working alone
Writing or editing	A competitive atmosphere
Listening to music	Being busy
Team sports	Working at home
Making people laugh	Physically demanding work
Teaching things to others	Intellectually challenging work
Solving problems	Being the boss

Create your own interest inventory. Make a list!

When making a list of your interests, ask the people closest to you if there's anything they would add to your list. Yes, nobody decides what your interests are except you; however, others may notice things you may have missed or even forgotten. For example, if your mother reminds you that when you were young you spent many hours creating Barbie doll houses and furniture out of the household recycling, you might realize that your old interest is still there, except in the grown-up world it might be called furniture design, interior decorating, or architecture.

In some cases, our greatest interests are very clear – they are the things we are already good at, and we've become good at them because the learning and the practice was *enjoyable* to us. And that's the key: pursuing something that interests you will make the learning and the practice a positive experience. And there will be lots of learning and practice ahead!

Pursuing your interests makes practice enjoyable

The truth is, hardly anyone is born with their career destiny already determined (unless perhaps you're a member of a royal family, which is pretty unlikely), so we all have to start from scratch to reach whatever goals interest us. Greta Thunberg didn't know how to fight climate change until she learned and practiced effective public speaking, but she clearly had an interest in doing so. Michael Jordan wasn't born a natural athlete, and wasn't even considered tall enough for basketball when he was young, but lots of determination and effort got him to his goal. Bill Gates didn't know how to build a computer platform until his interests and his surroundings led him to develop his skills and establish Microsoft.

Nearly any interest can lead toward future work, although the old saying "do what you love and the money will follow" doesn't specify the *amount* of money that will follow. That's something else to consider, just like it was when thinking about "passions." Are your potential career interests aligned with your future lifestyle interests? Being able to balance your interests (for career satisfaction) and your ability to generate income (to pay for food and shelter and more) is really a survival skill.

Questions to ask yourself:

- What do you enjoy learning about? What topics do you search for on the internet? What activities do you enjoy practicing?

- What is it about these things that makes them interesting for you?

- Is there something that sounds interesting to try or to learn about, but you haven't had the opportunity to do so yet?

- What kind of school assignments do you prefer doing? Essays, projects, hands-on? Why?

- What kind of environment do you prefer to be in? Why do you prefer this? Do you like being with small or large groups of people, or being alone? What kinds of people tend to bring out the best in you?

- What type of lifestyle do you envision for yourself in the future? What kind of income will you need to support this? Do you have a preference for where and how and when you will work?

Aptitudes

Your interests are usually pretty closely related to your **aptitudes**, which are the abilities you were born with – the talents that you have naturally, and may have inherited from your parents – or that you learned very early on in your life. They describe how you think and behave.

The list of aptitudes is vast! Here are some examples:

- *Talent or capability aptitudes* may make you naturally artistic, musical, spatial, kinesthetic, athletic, numerical, linguistic, strategic, imaginative, attentive, etc.
- *Social aptitudes* might mean that when dealing with others you tend to be introverted or extroverted, charismatic, empathetic, competitive, leading or managing, manipulative, communicative, inspiring, reasoning, etc.
- *Attitude or personality aptitudes* might include traits like being naturally optimistic or pessimistic, self-disciplined, organized, curious, adaptable, introspective, philosophical, creative, analytical, resilient, systematic, self-directed, rational, emotional, etc.

When you learn more about something or improve your ability, you are gaining knowledge and skills. It is much *easier* for you to develop knowledge and skills in areas where you already have a natural aptitude. For example, if you were born with a naturally strong awareness of patterns and relationships, you probably find math and physics easier to understand than someone without the same aptitude. If you were born with a good musical ear, it might not be difficult for you to learn to play an instrument or compose music. If you have inherited a knack for pulling bits and pieces together to make something new and useful, this aptitude might help you easily become skilled at auto mechanics, electrical engineering or industrial design.

Aptitudes can make learning easier

You are also more likely to show *interest* in activities for which you have a natural talent because they are relatively easy for you, and you are more likely to develop those talents even *further* if given the opportunity to use them. The better you get at it, the more you'll enjoy it, the more you'll practice, and the better you'll get... One doesn't *need* an innate talent to have an interest and develop knowledge or skill in a certain area, but having an aptitude for it often lays the groundwork. We're good at things that we like, and we like the things we're good at.

There are probably also lots of things that you might have an aptitude for, but you've never been exposed to them or had the chance to try them. Some people will discover later in life that they truly enjoy working with wood, or that they've got a knack for training animals, or that quantum physics makes a lot of sense to them. This is why it's a great idea to take advantage of any opportunity to learn something new – you never really know when your new learning or experience will come in handy in the future, or even lead you in a new direction.

Commander Chris Hadfield recommends that when an opportunity to learn something new presents itself, always take it! You never know when you might use that new something – it might end up having greater value than you expected as you walk the path to your goals. Read about Commander Hadfield's career journey to the Space Station in his book, An Astronaut's Guide to Life on Earth.10 Image from:
https://asc-csa.gc.ca/eng/multimedia/search/ image/watch/573

There are some online "career aptitude" tests that don't actually measure your aptitudes, but can still be useful tools in getting you to think about your career *interests*. They often require you to choose your preference between two activities or two types of job. If you had to choose between bricklaying and composing musical scores, would you be able to choose? How can you choose between two things you've probably never even tried? The idea with this kind of test is to think about the activities and environments involved with these two jobs: the bricklayer's work is largely physical, probably outdoors, building something structural and decorative; the composer's work is largely mental, probably indoors, creating something with musical language, instruments and electronic equipment. Which kind of work would appeal to you more?

There are also some better aptitude tests you may be able to do with a school or career counsellor. These are designed to measure traits such as creativity, problem-solving, and logical, linguistic and numerical reasoning. They are meant to predict your likelihood of success in various activities or careers, showing what kinds of work you might be good at if given the right training. The test results match the aptitudes you've shown with suitable career options, helping you think a little more deeply about the way your aptitudes might be related to your future job satisfaction.

Online vs. professional aptitude tests

Questions to ask yourself:

- What did you learn most easily in high school? Why was it easy for you?

- What are some of the aptitudes you already know you have? Can you think of any types of careers that require your particular aptitudes?

- What skills and knowledge will you need to add to that natural talent in order to develop it into consistently excellent performance?

Strengths and Weaknesses

Your personal strengths are closely connected to your aptitudes and your personality. Most people understand the meaning of having "strengths," although they don't necessarily recognize them in themselves. Your strengths are your *ways of being*: your ways of dealing with other people, managing your life, making changes, and manipulating your world. They are your thought and behaviour patterns. Your strengths reflect where you're at right now in your life, because they have affected, and been affected by, all your previous experiences.

Strengths develop from aptitudes and learning

Your strengths may be found in the aptitudes you have harnessed and further developed. Your strengths may also be certain thought patterns and ways of doing things that you have learned from the experiences you've had during your life. You may have strength in managing your attention and getting work done on time because you previously failed due to procrastination, so you then chose to learn about ways to control your focus and keep on top of deadlines to avoid repeating that mistake. Or perhaps you have strength in patient, active listening, because you have grown up with a family member with a developmental delay who needed calm and unhurried communication. You might have gained strength in learning new languages because your French immersion schooling helped you build on a natural aptitude for language comprehension.

Personal context influences your thinking & behaviour

So, your ways of being have their roots in your *personal context*, which is simply all those things in your life that have brought you to where you are right now. Your personal context may include things like your health, income, level of education, family situation, cultural background, gender, location, etc. – everything that adds up to your current life situation, and thus everything that adds up to the way you currently think and behave.

Other strengths that might be especially great to have in specific careers include things like persevering through difficulties, paying attention to details, doing things in an original way instead of following the crowd, loving learning, thinking logically to solve problems, communicating precisely, being assertive, focusing intently, following instructions carefully, or being ethically responsible.

The thought patterns and the ways of doing things that you have learned are not always in your best interest, of course. You may also have developed *weaknesses* that will hinder your success if you repeatedly think or act in a way that stifles your open-mindedness, creativity, motivation or effort. Attributes like procrastination, insecurity and disorganization generally cause difficulties in post-secondary, or in any career; sensitivity, multitasking or perfectionism, on the other hand, might be considered strengths in some careers but weaknesses in others. We often do recognize our weaknesses and how they hamper us, although we still don't necessarily act on them. Some bad habits are not easy to reverse, but everyone is able to change if they adjust their mindset and get help to start on a different road.

Your strengths, weaknesses and personal context are not only going to determine what you **want** to choose for your career, they're also going to affect what you are **able** to choose for your career. What you want and what you're able to do don't always match. You may *want* to become a doctor, but if your home life makes it impossible to consider spending the next ten years in university, then you may be better *able* to manage a different career. You may *want* to go to college, but if you're flat broke and don't qualify for financial aid and your marks were too low to earn a scholarship, you may not be *able* to register until you've worked for another year. On the other hand, you may *want* to go to university even though you're not *able* to move to attend campus, but you do have the initiative and the drive to seek out and attend a part-time online university program that meets your needs. Many people are able to overcome the difficulties that their personal contexts may present, especially if they are willing to look for information and accept help from educational and social services – a choice that shows signs of a growth mindset. Having a growth mindset is an awesome strength!

Again, there are strengths tests you can do online that may help you improve your self-awareness when searching for potential career directions. Some simple ones are free; some more comprehensive ones, like the CliftonStrengths 34, can be purchased online. If you can afford to have a comprehensive as-

Weaknesses

What you want to do vs. what you can do

sessment and review of your strengths, interests and/or aptitudes, meeting with a qualified career counsellor may be worthwhile.

Questions to ask yourself:

- What strengths are most characteristic of you? What brings out your best? As you think about the times when you've done well or handled something well, what were the ingredients of that success?

- Think about a challenge you've experienced in your life that you have overcome. What did you do to overcome that challenge? How did you do it? (This also reveals your strengths.)

- Do you recognize any weaknesses in yourself that might complicate or get in the way of your post-secondary or career success? Do you think you can make adjustments to correct this weakness, with help? Do you have the ability (the self-efficacy) to request this help?

- Do you feel that your personal context could hinder you from being able to pursue an interest that you have? If so, is there a way to use your strengths in pursuing this interest through a different path?

Values

Goals matching values leads to success

When considering different career options, it's important to do your research and have a good understanding of what your life would look like in that career. Your personal values play a big role in how satisfied you will be in the future. When it comes to making decisions – both the little day-to-day ones and the big life-changing ones – your core values can guide you toward actions that make you feel good about yourself. The stronger the link between your values and your goals, the more motivated and successful you are likely to be in achieving them.

What exactly are your values? There are general societal or cultural values that we grow up with that are meant to help us live together peacefully – a general morality or set of principles, those perceptions of what is right and what is wrong. But each person also has personal core values: their judgements of what's most important in their own life; their own principles or standards that guide their opinions, behaviour, and desires for the future. Most young people have some very strong values, but may not have really thought about them and pinned down what is most important to them. Pinning them down can actually help to clarify where you would like your life to go.

Core values guide your thoughts & actions

If you've never really thought about it before, then figuring out what your personal core values are will probably take some reflection. You can analyze your past experiences: at times when you've felt good about yourself, what did you do that brought on those positive emotions? Whatever it was, it was probably aligned with your personal values. On the other hand, your values kick in through your conscience, when you act in a way that isn't right for you – if you've ever felt badly about the way you've acted, it's because you haven't lived up to your own values. You might also try to name a person or fictional character that you admire, and think about the characteristics of that person that make you respect them.

Creating a list of your core values can be undertaken like a game of Battleship, exploring and reducing the targets until you only have to find that last cruiser or submarine. The following is a list of values, though it is by no means complete and you can add in any other values that have meaning for you. Look through the list and cross off, one by one, those values that are *less* important to you, until you end up with only five or six left. The ones that are left will represent your core values.

What are your core values?

Acceptance	Expertise	Kindness	Recognition
Adventure	Faith	Knowledge	Relationships
Balance	Fame	Leadership	Reputation
Beauty	Family	Learning	Respect
Boldness	Fitness	Loyalty	Responsibility
Caring	Freedom	Love	Safety
Challenge	Friendship	Making a Difference	Security
Change	Fun	Meaningful Work	Self-Respect
Community	Generosity	Modesty	Sensuality
Communication	Growth	Morality	Spirituality
Compassion	Happiness	Money	Status
Competence	Harmony	Nature	Strength

Competition	Health	Openness	Success
Cooperation	Helping Others	Originality	Teamwork
Connection	Honesty	Order	Thrill
Country	Humour	Patience	Trust
Courage	Imagination	Peace	Wellness
Creativity	Independence	Personal Expression	Winning
Democracy	Individuality	Pleasure	Wisdom
Diversity	Innovation	Power	Working Hard
Effectiveness	Integrity	Pride	_____
Entertainment	Intelligence	Privacy	_____
The Environment	Intuition	Professionalism	_____
Equality	Involvement	Prosperity	_____
Excellence	Justice	Quality	_____

Understanding how it feels to engage with your core values can directly affect the path you take toward a career. For example, if you highly value making connections with people, then you'll probably know that an online program or a career of remote work may not meet your needs because it doesn't match your core values. If you highly value knowledge and expertise, you might want to plan for a lengthy post-secondary journey, or consider a career that involves research or the sharing of your own knowledge. If freedom and independence are important to you, a career where you will be monitored or constrained by schedules or locations will probably prove to be frustrating. Clearly, it is essential to do in-depth research into the actual day-to-day activities and working environment of any career that sounds interesting to you.

Engage your core values!

Identifying and sticking to your values makes it much easier to find your direction, gain meaning and purpose for your life, and live up to your own expectations. Living according to your own personal values – not the ideals that bombard us through the media, social groups and other external influences – enhances your autonomy, character, and integrity.

Questions to ask yourself:

- What are your most important values?
- How will your top values be reflected in your career choice(s)? Is it important to you to make lots of money, to have a very stable job or a flexible one, to have regular busi-

ness hours, to work alone or with other people, to work from home, to help others, to travel...? Will the career(s) you're considering meet those values?

Parents' Note:
Encourage your child to explore their interests, aptitudes, strengths and values. Find some of the available online tests and surveys, and explore how your child's results are reflected in their attitudes and behaviours around work, learning and leisure. It is essential to remain non-judgemental, seeking only to help your child recognize and acknowledge their own characteristics and how they might help lead them toward or away from potential career directions.

You might want to explore your own at the same time – it might be interesting to talk about how people who are closely related, often with very similar personal contexts, can still be very different.

If your child is having great difficulty in narrowing down their initial career direction, you may want to ask for help from a guidance counsellor at your child's school. You might also consider seeking help from a reputable professional career counsellor. This is an expensive option, but these services are sometimes partially covered through employee extended health care benefits.

What Are You Aiming For?

Once you've got *yourself* somewhat figured out – or at least you're on the road to that – you're ready to start figuring out your next steps.

When you've got some ideas for career directions that sound interesting, or perhaps even a specific idea for a career you want to pursue, you can follow that up with some job research. Where could this idea lead you? What would this career actually look like? Do the education, employment opportunities and work conditions suit you? You will want to get a well-rounded view of any potential careers before setting a course toward them.

Job research

Your job research can uncover the answers to questions like these:

1. The Work Itself: What kind of work might you end up doing? What does this kind of career entail? What is the workday like when you have this kind of job?
2. Employment: How easy would it be to find a job? How much are you likely to get paid? Where would you need to live?
3. Required Education: What kinds of skills would you need to perform a job like this? How would you become qualified? Would you need to attend a college, a private institution, a university? Where? For how long? How much would that cost?
4. Other Options: Are there other careers that are similar or related to this one? If so, are any of them more appealing in some way?

Even without a future career plan, getting more information about all the different kinds of work out there might actually turn up something intriguing. On the other hand, learning more about different jobs might make you want to cross some off your list – also good to know!

If you are in high school, the guidance or student services department at your school may have set you up with an account for a program such as Career Cruising (also known as Xello), which keeps track of your school accomplishments and includes assessment tools and occupation profiles to help you learn about different careers. Some colleges and universities also offer online career exploration tools like this for their post-secondary students.

Looking through the programs available from Ontario's colleges and universities, you might get some ideas for potential careers related to your interests. You might also find some intriguing options among the many possibilities that you didn't even know existed. Information about the thousands of college and university programs in Ontario can be found in Chapter 4.

There are a myriad of websites describing endless jobs, but be sure to use only Canadian sites to get accurate information, since the education, responsibilities and working conditions of some careers are different here than they are outside of Canada. A safe bet is the government of Canada's Job Bank website, which includes a Career Planning tool where you can research the skills, wages and job prospects of a huge number of careers, province by province (https://www.jobbank.gc.ca/career-planning).

[margin: Career Planning tool on Job Bank]

Knowing about the reliability of employment in any careers that interest you is certainly helpful. For example, the fields of health, technology and skilled trades all continue to expand rapidly, with almost unlimited opportunities; work in another sector may be much less abundant, but your interest and motivation might make it the most meaningful and worthwhile route to follow. You need to be fully aware of your future job prospects from the get-go. There are a couple of other Ontario government sites that can help you understand what jobs are in demand. Learn about the labour market in different regions of Ontario and also find some job profiles at https://www.ontario.ca/page/labour-market. If you're considering a career that requires going to college, you can also check to see if your career direction matches with recent job trends by exploring with the Labour Market search tool, available at https://www.app.tcu.gov.on.ca/eng/labourmarket/employmentprofiles/index.asp.

[margin: Labour market research tools]

You'll find many other resources out there to give you an idea of what it's like to have a specific job. Just keep in mind that data is really useful, but it doesn't always tell the whole story. For instance, data might show that being a Personal Support Worker does not pay as well as some other occupations, but that there is a high employment rate for graduates; some missing information might also be important to you, such as the fact that it takes less than a year to earn your certificate, or that many employers offer only part-time work, or that the emotional satisfaction from this type of work makes it a great fit for certain people.

An excellent way to find out more about a potential career is to talk with the people who have worked in the profession that interests you. If there is someone in your family, or even a friend of a friend of a friend who has some experience in a similar job, then let them know you'd like to ask some questions

Get more information from people employed in that field

about it. Almost anyone will be more than happy to tell you what they know. Your high school guidance counsellors may be able to guide you toward a working professional, or the program advisors at a college or university may be able to connect you to a working graduate of their program – these people can describe the reality of their jobs. Contacting a related professional association (for example, the Ontario Association of Veterinary Technicians, or Trial Lawyers, or Conservation Officers) may also result in you finding a mentor who can give you current information about both the positive and negative aspects of a career that interests you.

The more you know about yourself, the more likely you are to make choices that will lead to a fulfilling career – the work you do will better match your interests, aptitudes, strengths and values. If you can figure out a type of work that is likely to build your feelings of self-worth and satisfaction, you will be off to a great start on your career journey.

Questions to ask yourself:

- Have you come up with one or more ideas for an initial career direction that sounds interesting to you?

- Did your job research clarify the typical day-to-day work, employment conditions and required education for a particular career that interests you? Did this increase or decrease your interest in that career?

- Did your research turn up any new directions that might be worth looking into?

- Do you know anyone who could give you their personal insight into what their career is like? Have you asked your school's guidance department for help in making connections, or sent questions to any professional organizations related to the careers that interest you?

Parents' Note:
Take the time to help your child explore the ins and outs of future careers that might interest them, if you are able. Talk to other parents about what their jobs are like. What kinds of work do their adult children do? If your child expresses an interest in a particular career, see if you can find someone currently working in that field who might be able to answer their questions, or even act as a mentor for them. Even if you are not able to help in this way, your enthusiasm and open-mindedness toward the possibilities will help pave the way toward your child's initial career choices.

There are many new fields and new kinds of employment that have been established over the past couple of decades, and change happens so quickly now that many more newfangled careers will be created in the decade to come. We cannot even predict what jobs will be available for your child in the future!

3

WHEN YOU DON'T FEEL READY
(You have other options)

What if you still haven't gotten yourself or your future figured out? Should you pursue post-secondary education or not?

No reasonable person would advocate going to school just for the sake of going. Spending years working on a "whatever" degree or diploma without any goals, just because going is expected of you, would be a very costly and potentially ineffective pastime... though, of course, no learning is ever really in vain. Simply having earned a certificate, diploma or degree is proof to future employers that you are able to learn and achieve success at a post-secondary level – you will clearly have plenty of transferable skills. Even realizing what you do *not* want to do as a career is a valuable lesson, particularly if you come to this conclusion after only one or two years of schooling. This realization may prevent years of expense and work in a career that might leave you unsatisfied.

Remember, you're only making decisions about what do *now*, what direction to go *first*. Most people can expect to change jobs and even careers many times – Canadians now average 10-15 job changes and 2-3 career changes during their working lives[11] – so you don't have to plan out your whole life, or even stick with whatever plans you make today. Things change, and so will you. It may be better to focus your energy on simply figuring out your first step, and then just let life happen. The future can be hard to predict anyway, so you might want to stick to relatively short-term goals and see where they take you. Flexibility is key in the world of work today, so why not start practicing it now?

If you're not sure which career directions interest you or what your logical next steps should be, there are still a number of

Short-term, flexible goals

avenues open to you. Perhaps you should simply think about what changes you can make that may lead you to new ideas or a better understanding of yourself. Change will help you to grow. Maintaining the status quo will probably not get you anywhere. On the other hand, with every life change and new experience you'll have the opportunity to meet new people, try something new, expand or improve your skills, get to know the world and how it works, and develop emotionally, socially and intellectually.

All new experiences = growth

So just do *something*.

The following are some of your *other* options.

The "Victory Lap"

If you have not yet completed high school, then earning your Ontario Secondary School Diploma (OSSD) will be an essential first step. It will be much more difficult to achieve a sustainable and satisfactory career of stable work that earns more than minimum wage without an OSSD (though not impossible, if you have an exceptional talent or are extremely skilled in a high-demand activity).

Taking an extra year of secondary school to earn credits beyond the 30 required for graduation is not uncommon. There are several worthwhile reasons to do a "victory lap." You may want to take courses you had not previously considered or had not been able to schedule. You may have developed an interest in a new subject area and need to take the courses required for entry into a particular post-secondary program.

Reasons for a victory lap

If you're planning to spend an extra year in high school to give yourself more time to pinpoint an appropriate post-secondary program, you may want to consider trying something a little bit outside the box. Most Ontario high schools offer co-op programs, which actually give you high school credits for spending part of your day working in the community. You may not be paid, but you will gain valuable experience working in a position that appeals to you, learning more about that field and adding it to your résumé. In fact, if you are interested in a skilled trade, a co-op course taken in high school can give you a head

Co-ops

start in an apprenticeship program, through registration with OYAP, the Ontario Youth Apprenticeship Program (https://oyap.com/). Your school counsellors or co-op coordinator can give you more information about this. You can also read more about apprenticeships in Chapter 4.

Dual credits

Alternately, many schools offer dual-credit programs, whereby high school students can attend certain college classes and earn *both* high school and college credits. This is another great way to test out the waters of a potential future career direction. Read more at https://www.ontario.ca/page/dual-credit-programs, then talk to your school counsellor to see if this option is available to you.

Choosing to pass an extra year in high school simply because you don't know what else to do, or because you just want to play school sports, would not be a growth-minded plan – this would only continue the status quo, not offering the new life and learning experiences that benefit your personal growth. If you're still feeling unsure, the suggestions that follow may be more productive options for you.

Parents' Note:

If your child wants to return to high school, explore the reasons why, and how this might benefit them or hold them back. Examine the situation objectively: will they spend the year productively, with an interest or need for new learning and some different experiences, or will the year pass with little change and little new intellectual and emotional growth? Working with your child and the school's guidance department, determine the purpose of the coming year and create a plan or a contract based on a combination of educational, work and leisure endeavours that will foster your child's self-awareness and maturity.

Ensure, as well, that you have not influenced your child's decision to stay in high school simply to meet your own emotional needs as a parent who is afraid to let their child move on. This is not uncommon, but is not in your child's best interest.

Questions to ask yourself:

- Do you have good reasons to do another year of high school? Do you need to earn additional credits or want to explore a new interest?

- Would doing a co-op or taking a dual credit course benefit you?

The Work World

Gap Year, Part 1

For students, a "gap year" is generally known as a one-year plan to work or volunteer within your community or as a member of a national or international program, usually with an expectation of following through on post-secondary education afterward. A gap year may be seen as an opportunity to explore life and learn new skills by trying out different types of work, working with or helping others and becoming part of a new community, traveling, or simply opening up to new experiences. Time spent in purposeful experiential living leads to social and emotional growth, increased responsibility, self-regulation and self-efficacy, and can be downright life-changing!

Work, travel, or volunteer

Often, young people take a gap year (or gap semester or gap multiple-years) for a simple, practical reason: to work and earn enough money to pay for their future educational costs. This is a totally valid rationale at a time when the cost of post-secondary education is very high. Both the "Heading to Work" section that follows this and the "Paying For It" section in Chapter 5 have information about finding jobs for youth.

If a gap year of work is your plan, consider also expanding your perspective in other ways during your year of work, such as volunteering in the community, trying out a new hobby or club, or exploring your region. Make the year a meaningful one in more ways than just your bank account.

An excellent resource is the Canadian Gap Year Association, a non-profit organization that offers information, certifications, and even personal coaching to help you plan for a valuable year

Canadian Gap Year Association

that meets your financial needs and expands your outlook on life (https://www.cangap.ca/).

Questions to ask yourself:

- If you expect to spend a gap year working before proceeding to post-secondary, have you thought about what kind of working experience would benefit you most in relation to your future career direction?
- If you simply want to work to earn money for future needs, have you prepared your résumé and looked at the kinds of jobs available in your area?
- Have you explored the resources offered by your nearest employment centre and made an appointment with an employment counsellor?

Heading to Work

Entering the work world without any expectation of pursuing further education is also a suitable path for some people. Perhaps higher education does not interest you – avoiding further schooling at this point in life is a perfectly legitimate choice. It is also quite common to spend many years working full-time, and find much later in life that you have a desire or a need to change careers. Rest assured, your post-secondary opportunities will still be there for you in the future. In the meantime, there are plenty of jobs for high school graduates, and not all of them involve flipping burgers.

At current pay rates and depending on your living costs, a minimum wage job will not afford you any luxuries. On the other hand, you may have the inside scoop on a more lucrative, full-time position with a company that offers opportunities for future advancement, or you might have a strength or skill that you can put to use in creating your own business. Going straight to full-time work is a very satisfactory route to success for many Canadians.

Employment prep and job search tools

The Ontario government lists a variety of employment programs for teens through to post-secondary graduates; you might qualify for several of them (htttps://www.ontario.ca/page/get-help-finding-youth-or-student-job). They also provide some preparation and job search resources for anyone looking for employment (https://www.ontario.ca/page/jobs-and-employment). An appointment with a government employment counsellor can be very beneficial, as they can assess your skills, help you write a résumé, prepare for interviews and assist with your job search. Find the employment centre closest to you with the search tool at https://feat.findhelp.ca/.

Parents' Note:
Your child's desire to move directly into full-time employment instead of continuing with their education after high school can be seen as a very responsible choice. Not only will they earn a living, but they will also learn about managing their finances and, potentially, save up enough for future post-secondary expenses should they choose to apply later. Spending some time employed in lower-paid and precarious jobs that are commonly available to high school graduates will give your child time to experience the rigours and responsibilities of daily existence, and time to figure out their next steps. They may come to appreciate higher education and the opportunities it provides.

Questions to ask yourself:
- Would you prefer to enter the workforce than to continue in school? If so, do you have a plan for the type of work you would like to get into?
- Have you found the nearest employment office, and do you plan to make an appointment with an employment counsellor?

Post-secondary Preparatory Programs

Even if you haven't exactly figured out what you want to do, there may be a post-secondary program that will act as a *transition* toward something else.

General and Career Foundation Certificate Programs

Many colleges offer short introductory or preparatory programs that allow you to test the waters of a certain program type, narrow down your goals, and earn a certificate before diving into a full diploma program. Usually lasting for two semesters, these "pre-" certificates may give you a very general understanding of subjects through programs such as pre-health, trades, business, media, technology, community services, dance, theatre, etc.

Preparatory programs

If you don't have all the eligibility requirements for direct admission to a diploma program, a general introductory program may earn you the credits you need to get there. If you already have an idea for a program you'd like to get into afterward, be very careful to ensure that your general introductory program will meet its admission requirements. For example, if you plan to take a pre-health program at one college to help you get into a healthcare program at a different college, check to make sure that your future healthcare program will accept this pre-health certificate as fulfilling their prerequisites.

General and Year 1 programs

A general arts and sciences program is offered at many colleges, and a general Year 1 in a faculty like arts or science is available at several universities. A year spent in this kind of general program allows students to explore their interests and experience college learning while figuring out what career direction they want to take. It also gives students time to learn and practice the academic skills necessary at the post-secondary level, such as researching, writing, critiquing, groupwork, etc.; assessing and exercising their self-regulatory behaviours; and simply getting comfortable with the post-secondary environment, routines, and atmosphere overall.

Foundational certificates

In addition, more specific or targeted preparatory or foundational programs and certificates are offered in a wide variety of fields, both in colleges and in the Continuing Education departments of universities. They can last from mere weeks to one or two years. This type of program offers a more focused experience within a specific area that already interests you – a foundation, or basic understanding – without the years required to achieve a diploma or degree. It will also prepare you for further study if you end up choosing that route. Many foundational programs or certifications can steer you directly into employment. You may find foundational certificate programs in areas such as art, aviation, business, carpentry, community and child studies, computers, culinary arts, dance, design, electrical, firefighting, health, hospitality, Indigenous studies, child services, mechanical, media, motive power, music, technology, theatre, and more. The offerings at Ontario public and private colleges may change year by year.

Academic Upgrading

If you did not complete high school and receive an Ontario Secondary School Diploma (OSSD), you may need to earn a grade 12 "equivalency" with a General Education Development certificate (GED) in order to be admitted into a college or university program. Anyone can take a GED test online if they wish. The Ontario government's upgrading options for adult learners can be found at https://www.ontario.ca/page/adult-learning. *[GED test]*

Students sometimes want to take new high school courses or repeat courses they've previously passed, if they need a specific course or a better mark to get into a post-secondary program. Though not free, anyone can accomplish this through inexpensive online courses from TVO ILC (https://www.ilc.org) or another online platform that is accepted by your future college or university. Students who upgrade in this manner must have access to a computer and reliable internet service. As well, be prepared to set and meet time lines for completion of the course. *[Virtual High School courses]*

You can also take a *free*, personalized academic upgrading program specifically to improve your skills in English, math, science, writing, computers, etc., to help you enter a post-secondary program or simply to improve your employability. These Academic Career Entrance (ACE) courses can be taken individually or as part of a certificate program, either online (https://www.acedistancedelivery.ca/) or on-campus at most Ontario colleges. Learn more at the ACE website (https://www.ontario.ca/page/adult-learning-academic-career-entrance). The Ontario Colleges website also has links to each college's upgrading program (https://www.ontariocolleges.ca/en/news/resources-for-college-preparation). *[Academic Career Entrance (ACE)]*

Questions to ask yourself:

- Are you unsure of your post-secondary path and/or your readiness for college or university?

- Have you considered the benefits of taking a general or foundational program to test the waters while developing your skills and building your confidence?

- If you did not graduate from high school, would taking a GED test or enrolling in an Academic Career Entrance (ACE) course be a good first step on the path to higher education?

Travel

Gap Year, Part 2

A "gap year" for many young people has the prospect of adventure: experiencing new environments, encountering different ways of being and thinking, and building connections. This kind of exploration is both external (physical) and internal (psychological), and often involves travel. You might be thinking about working and living with extended family members in another community, working as a server or an au pair in another country, or volunteering with a service organization on another continent. Or, at this point, you may only be thinking about the places around the globe that you want to visit – so much to see and so little time!

Travelling in Canada or internationally presents myriad opportunities for unique and meaningful experiences, getting to know and understand the diversity of people and places in our world, and resulting in personal growth and development in so many areas. Of course, time spent travelling must be well-planned and organized to ensure that you remain physically, mentally and financially well, and that you feel your time is being spent effectively and productively. You'll need to consider the cost, who you might be with, where you're going to stay, whether you're legally able to work, how you'll find employment, and how you're going to get around, etc. Depending on your plan, you may need specific items of clothing or safety equipment; travel, work or study visas in your passport; vacci-

[margin note: Planning for travel]

nations; a roaming phone plan; or even some new language preparation. Simply planning for your travels can be an enlightening experience in itself.

An online search will show that there are many businesses that manage national and international cultural, language and academic travel for young adults, as well as many organizations that mobilize youth to help improve the physical and social conditions in developing countries. Carefully research any organization you're considering, and bear in mind that going with a Canadian-based organization is likely to be the least complicated. In addition to their gap year planning and guidance services, CanGap also offers a database of reliable travel-based gap year programs (https://www.cangap.ca/).

Volunteer organizations

Before leaving on your travel adventure, be sure to make note of any details and application deadlines you might need to stick to if your goal is to enter a post-secondary program upon your return. Have any necessary paperwork already completed and ready to go, if possible, or at least make all the required application information easy to access from afar when the time comes. Staying aware of developments and schedules still happening back home will prevent any future disappointments.

Far from being a year spent delaying your post-secondary progress, travel and other "worldly" experiences are often considered an advantage when applying to competitive programs. It is well understood that these kinds of enriching experiences boost future students' self-awareness, self-efficacy and overall maturity, and thus are looked upon very favourably.

Questions to ask yourself:

- Do you have a goal for a gap year that involves travelling in Canada or elsewhere? How much time do you have the logistic and financial ability to spend travelling?

- Have you researched the various opportunities for travel and volunteerism offered by reputable organizations?

- Are you prepared to create a detailed plan for the year to ensure a positive experience?

4

WHERE DOES YOUR FUTURE LIE?
(Making choices about learning)

If you have an idea about something you might like to study, where would you study it? What are your post-secondary options? What's out there?

There are many different ways to achieve a post-secondary education that will lead you to a successful and satisfying career. The admission requirements for each institution will vary, and the requirements for individual programs will be different. The type of learning that will take place within a program can differ as well. You need to find the right fit for you.

The post-secondary landscape has changed greatly over the past couple of decades: the dividing line between offerings at colleges, universities and other post-secondary institutions has blurred.

Until relatively recently, most high school students could easily determine the type of post-secondary institution that would best meet their career expectations. For example, going to university in Canada meant following a theoretical or professional program (arts, humanities, sciences or engineering, for example) that was often expected to earn you a well-paid, white-collar position in a large company. Going to college meant training for a technical or service career (like plumbing, mechanics, culinary or hairstyling) through a program with lower entrance requirements, and resulting in a job that likely paid less but was more hands-on. Private post-secondary institutions offered mostly religious or basic administrative programs. That has changed over the last twenty years and, as you will see, these easy classifications are definitely no longer the case.

As you research potential programs at potential post-secondary institutions, be sure to keep track of the information you find about specific programs and schools you're considering. All of these details are most useful when compiled in a list, table or spreadsheet of some sort, so it will be easy to compare the benefits and drawbacks of each program and school. Bringing all the information together in one spot will definitely simplify the process of making decisions later on.

Record your information

So what learning options are available now for Ontario's post-secondary students?

Colleges

Ontario's 27 public Colleges of Applied Arts and Technology and College Institutes of Technology house over 900 programs in Ontario, generally offering 1- or 2-year certificates, 2-year diplomas, 3-year advanced diplomas, graduate certificates, and apprenticeship programs. Some colleges also offer their own degree programs, or joint-degree programs in conjunction with a university. Many college programs include experiential learning through unpaid internships or practicums, and some colleges also offer co-op programs, which provide opportunities for paid, program-related work experience. There are two French-language Ontario colleges. Although college typically starts in September, many offer winter or spring starts for certain programs.

Many of Ontario's colleges have established smaller "extension" or "satellite" campuses in different locations, sometimes in conjunction with a different institution, in order to expand students' access to specific programs. When considering a college program, be sure to confirm exactly where (i.e., on which campus) that program will take place.

Information about Ontario's public colleges is available at www.OntarioColleges.ca. This site offers lots of great background on college admissions, tuition fees and financial aid, career information, program comparisons, and other resources. You can easily access individual college websites through the links from the "programs" and "colleges" search engines, and find them with the interactive map of the colleges' locations

Ontario Colleges information site

(https://www.ontariocolleges.ca/en/colleges/college-map). The guidance or student services office at your high school might also have paperback copies of each Ontario college's program catalogue (often called a "lookbook" or "viewbook"), which is often a better way to discover the huge variety of different programs on offer in the province. If they're not available at your school, the colleges will be happy to mail their information to you.

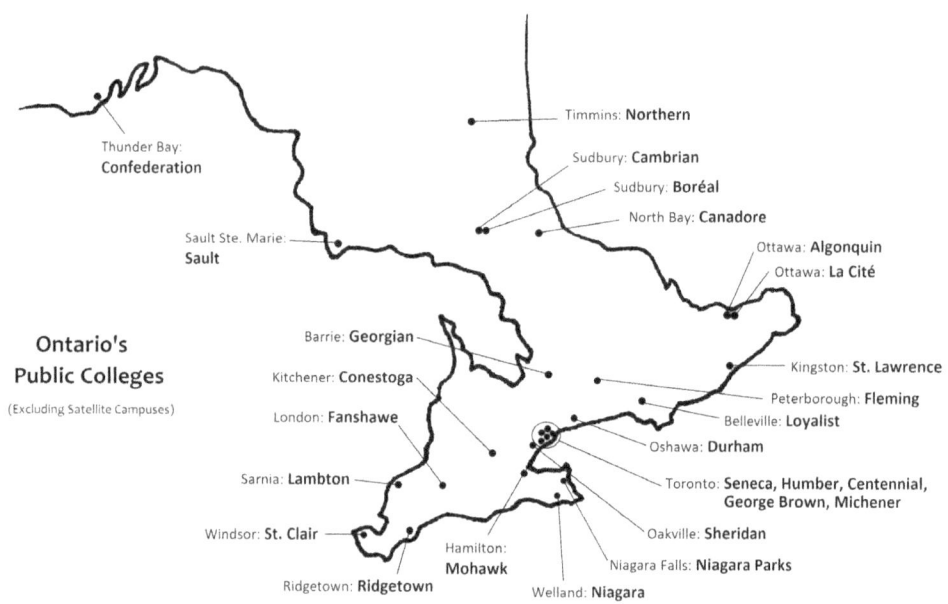

Universities

There are 21 universities in Ontario. They offer undergraduate degree programs at general (3-year), major (4-year) and honours (4-year) levels, as well as professional programs like law and medicine, and graduate programs (Masters, PhD) that require the completion of an honours-level degree for admission. Some university programs include experiential work placements through unpaid internships or practicums, and many offer co-op options for paid, program-related work experience.

Seven Ontario universities present some or all of their programs in French. Some universities also offer winter or spring admissions to certain programs.

Like the colleges, several of Ontario's universities have established smaller "satellite" campuses in different regions. Be sure to clarify the location of any program you're interested in.

As a university student, you can choose a major (the subject you want to focus on) that is fairly general or is quite specific. Some students focus on more than one subject by designating a double-major, or a major and a minor (a second subject, with a less intense focus). Applicants who are not ready to choose a major might prefer one of the universities that offers a "general first year" program in arts or science, allowing them to try a broader range of courses initially. Some universities have "interdisciplinary" and/or "self-directed" programs that may be broader or more specific, for those whose interests do not quite fit into one of the programs already offered. You may also find university programs that offer the option of spending one or two semesters studying abroad at a "sister" university.

Ontario Universities Info site

The Ontario Universities Information website (https://www.OntarioUniversitiesInfo.ca/) offers detailed information about each university's programs as well as tips on applying for and financing your studies, and the dates of the Ontario Universities Fair and virtual open houses. Again, another great way to discover what's out there is by looking through the universities' individual "viewbooks," which might be available through your high school's guidance or student services office, or accessed through a download or request form on the universities' websites. These make for very interesting reading – you'll probably discover programs that you've never even imagined, and some of them just might pique your interest!

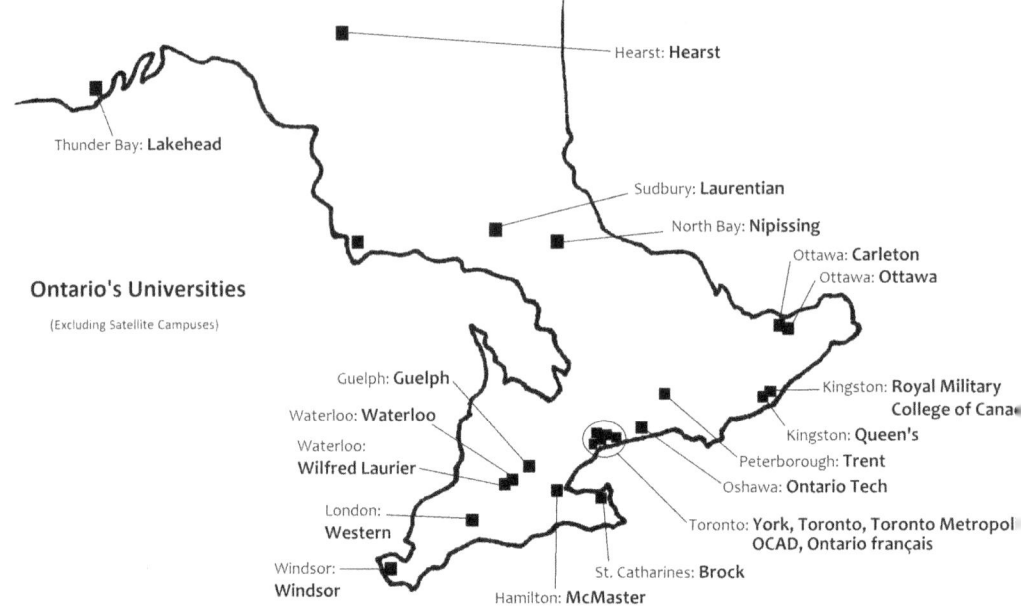

Military Careers and the Royal Military College of Canada

In addition to the combat and security work of the army, navy and air force that we think of as military careers, the Canadian Armed Forces (CAF) hire and train for an extensive array of full-time and part-time jobs in administration, health care, engineering, trades, technology, etc. Both full-time jobs in the regular forces and part-time jobs in the reserves offer training, competitive salaries, health benefits and paid vacation time. In order to join the CAF as a new recruit, you must be a Canadian citizen who is at least 18 years old (or 16, with parental permission) and have completed at least grade 10. When accepted, you will undergo basic training, which includes fitness, military, first aid and ethics training, before beginning the education specific to your military career. You can explore all the offerings of the CAF on their website: https://forces.ca/en/.

Paid education through the Canadian Armed Forces

The Armed Forces also offer paid education opportunities for eligible students interested in one of their college, university, Indigenous pre-university, or specialized programs. These programs pay for your tuition, books and equipment, as well as providing a salary and benefits while you study. Students are enrolled in the CAF, and, upon completion, will serve two months of military employment for each month of paid education. The CAF website provides more information (https://forces.ca/en/paid-education/).

One route for the CAF's paid education program is through the Royal Military College (RMC) in Kingston, a military-based university (https://www.rmc-cmr.ca/en). RMC grants both undergraduate and graduate degrees in a number of social science and humanities, science and engineering disciplines, all of which will include athletic, military and language study components. A diploma or degree can also be completed through another post-secondary institution if the desired program is not offered at RMC. RMC applications are due earlier than for other universities, and must be submitted through the Canadian Armed Forces website; information on applying is available at https://www.rmc-cmr.ca/en/registrars-office/apply-now. RMC entrance is very competitive, with an application process that is quite rigorous. Be prepared to spend some time on it.

Private Colleges

Career Colleges

Private career colleges, sometimes called "trade schools," offer certificate and diploma programs of varying durations. Private college programs are often based on local community or workforce needs, or on specific careers not well-represented by public colleges. There are over 400 private colleges in Ontario, where students are trained for careers that vary from the vocational trades, business and health fields to aesthetics, technology, tourism, and beyond. You may find private college programs that are very intense and lead quickly to workforce readiness. Their offerings are often more flexible than those of public institutions, with greater personalization, more frequent start dates, and more condensed schedules that lead to quick graduation.

Depending on the institution and program, students at private colleges may or may not qualify for government loans and grants (OSAP) to fund their education, though some private colleges have financial aid options of their own. Private colleges' programs must be approved by and registered with the provincial government to ensure their quality standards. You can search for registered and provincially-approved private career colleges in Ontario by location or by program through the database available at https://www.ontario.ca/page/private-career-colleges. Data about graduation, employment and satisfaction rates at the private colleges can be downloaded from http://www.tcu.gov.on.ca/pepg/audiences/pcc/#kpi.

margin note: Search for registered private colleges

Indigenous Institutes

Nine Indigenous Institutes across Ontario offer certificates, diplomas, degrees and/or apprenticeships in community and culture-based, Indigenous-governed post-secondary institutions, often in Indigenous languages. These programs may be offered in conjunction with a non-Indigenous college or university. Links to these Institutes are available at https://iicontario.ca/indigenous-institutes/ or https://www.ontario.ca/page/indigenous-institutes.

margin note: Indigenous Institutes

Faith-based Institutions

There are also a number of private, faith-based colleges and universities in Ontario. Most focus on theological or religious subjects, though some offer a broader variety of certificates, diplomas and degrees. You may notice that some Ontario universities have also incorporated small, faith-based "colleges" as part of their structure, although there are no specific religious beliefs or activities required of their applicants. You can find links to Ontario's faith-based colleges on the Ontario government's website: https://www.ontario.ca/page/private-postsecondary-schools.

margin note: Faith-based schools

Apprenticeships

An apprenticeship involves paid, on-the-job training combined with some classroom learning, to earn qualifications in the areas of industrial, construction, motive power and service trades. Many of the 144 skilled trades are consistently in high demand and lead to high job security and wages after a two- to five-year apprenticeship process. Indeed, some predict that about 40% of jobs in Ontario will be in the skilled trades by 2025[12].

SERVICE SECTOR

Aboriginal Child Development Practitioner
Agricultural-Dairy Herdsperson
Agricultural-Fruit Grower
Agricultural-Swine Herdsperson
Appliance Service Technician
Arborist
Assistant Cook
Baker
Baker-Patissier
Chef
Child & Youth Worker
Child Development Practitioner
Cook
Developmental Services Worker
Educational Assistant
Electronic Service Technician
Gemsetter/Goldsmith
Hairstylist
Horse Groom
Horse Harness Maker
Horticultural Technician
Information Technology-Contact Centre Customer Service Agent
Information Technology-Contact Centre Technical Support Agent
Information Technology-Hardware Technician
Information Technology-Network Technician
Institutional Cook
Micro Electronics Manufacturer
Native Clothing & Crafts Artisan
Network Cabling Specialist
Parts Technician
Retail Meat Cutter
Saddlery
Special Events Coordinator
Utility Arborist

CONSTRUCTION SECTOR

Architectural Glass & Metal Technician
Brick & Stone Mason
Cement (Concrete) Finisher
Concrete Pump Operator
Construction Boilermaker
Construction Craft Worker
Construction Millwright
Drywall Finisher & Plasterer
Drywall, Acoustic & Lathing Applicator
Electrician-Construction & Maintenance
Electrician-Domestic & Rural
Exterior Insulated Finish Systems Mechanic
Floor Covering Installer
General Carpenter
Hazardous Materials Worker
Heat & Frost Insulator
Heavy Equipment Operator-Dozer
Heavy Equipment Operator-Excavator
Heavy Equipment Operator-Tractor

Loader Backhoe
Hoisting Engineer-Mobile Crane Operator 1
Hoisting Engineer-Mobile Crane Operator 2
Hoisting Engineer-Tower Crane Operator
Iron Worker-Generalist
Iron Worker-Structural & Ornamental
Native Residential Construction Worker
Painter & Decorator-Commercial & Residential
Painter & Decorator-Industrial
Plumber
Powerline Technician
Precast Concrete Erector
Precast Concrete Finisher
Refractory Mason

Refrigeration & Air Conditioning Systems Mechanic
Reinforcing Rodworker
Residential (Low Rise) Sheet Metal Installer
Residential Air Conditioning Systems Mechanic
Restoration Mason
Roofer
Sheet Metal Worker
Sprinkler & Fire Protection Installer
Steamfitter
Terrazzo Tile & Marble Setter

INDUSTRIAL SECTOR

Bearings Mechanic
Blacksmith
Cabinetmaker
Computer Numerical Control (CNC) Programmer
Die Designer
Draftsperson-Mechanical
Draftsperson-Plastic Mould Design
Draftsperson-Tool & Die Design
Electric Motor System Technician
Electrician (Signal Maintenance)
Elevating Devices Mechanic
Entertainment Industry Power Technician
Facilities Mechanic
Facilities Technician
General Machinist
Hydraulic/Pneumatic Mechanic
Industrial Electrician
Industrial Mechanic Millwright
Instrumentation & Control Technician
Light Rail Overhead Contact Systems Linesperson
Locksmith
Machine Tool Builder & Integrator
Metal Fabricator (Fitter)

Mould Designer
Mould Maker
Mould or Die Finisher
Optics Technician (Lens & Prism Maker)
Packaging Machine Mechanic
Pattern Maker
Pressure Systems Welder
Process Operator-Food Manufacturing
Process Operator-Power
Process Operator-Refinery, Chemical & Liquid Processes
Process Operator-Wood Products
Railway Car Technician
Relay & Instrumentation Technician
Saw Filer/Fitter
Surface Blaster
Surface Mount Assembler
Thin Film Technician
Tool & Cutter Grinder
Tool & Die Maker
Tool & Gauge Inspector
Tool/Tooling Maker
Tractor-Trailer Commercial Driver
Water Well Driller
Welder

MOTIVE POWER SECTOR

Agricultural Equipment Technician
Alignment & Brakes Technician
Autobody & Collision Damage Repairer
Autobody Repairer
Automotive Electronic Accessory Technician
Automotive Glass Technician
Automotive Painter
Automotive Service Technician
Marine Engine Technician
Motive Power Machinist
Motorcycle Technician
Powered Lift Truck Technician
Recreation Vehicle Technician
Small Engine Technician
Transmission Technician
Truck & Coach Technician
Truck-Trailer Service Technician
Turf Equipment Technician

Skilled Trades Ontario provides detailed information about the trades, trade-related jobs and the apprenticeship process for each trade. Click on any of the 144 trades listed at https://www.ontario.ca/page/explore-trades-ontario#section-2 to learn more.

Twenty-three of the skilled trades are designated "compulsory" – in order to work in these trades, you must be a registered apprentice or have passed the required exam to become a certified tradesperson, and be a member of the Ontario College of Trades (a regulatory organization). The "non-compulsory" trades also have apprenticeship programs, but they do not all require a certification exam in order to work. Red Seal trades are governed by provincial law, to maintain a national standard of knowledge for those trades across Canada (http://www.red-seal.ca/trades/tr.1d.2s_1.3st-eng.html).

An apprenticeship can be started in three different ways:

1. Ontario colleges offer certificate and diploma programs related to the skilled trades, with the apprentice's earnings from their work periods covering much of their expenses during their sessions on campus (https://www.ontariocolleges.ca/en/apply/skilled-trades). Some trades foundations programs ("pre-trades" or "trades fundamentals") expose you to several different trades, if you're not sure which one best suits your interests. Free pre-apprenticeship training may also be available through some Ontario colleges if you

How to start an apprenticeship

qualify for this Ontario government program, whether you've graduated from high school or not (https://www.ontario.ca/page/prepare-apprenticeship).

2   As mentioned earlier, high school students in grades 11 and 12 can earn college credits toward an apprenticeship through work placements with the Ontario Youth Apprenticeship Program (OYAP) or Dual Credit programs. Your high school guidance department can arrange for this. Learn more at https://oyap.com/.

3   Find an employer or a sponsor who agrees to train you and pay for the work you will do during your apprenticeship. There are many loans and grants available for both employers and apprentices to cover the cost of wages, classes and tools. Employment Ontario can help match prospective apprentices with interested employers (https://www.ontario.ca/page/jobs-and-employment). Once an apprenticeship is agreed upon, you can officially apply online and then register as an apprentice with the Ontario College of Trades.

Inter-Provincial and International Options

Perhaps you're keen to explore life outside of Ontario, or even outside of Canada, as a component of your post-secondary education. There are many possibilities for learning in different programs and facilities (and also different languages) outside of our province, and they may offer attractive and worthy experiences as you journey in your new direction. If studying further afield is appealing but not practical for you at this point, keep in mind that these kinds of alternative routes may still be there for you in the future.

As a Canadian, you are free to travel and study in all parts of Canada. As an out-of-province applicant, however, you may face somewhat stiffer competition for available post-secondary spots in the other nine provinces and three territories. Colleges and universities prioritize students within their province over out-of-province and international students. That's not to say that acceptance into a school outside of Ontario will be difficult, it just depends what program you're keen on, and where you want to go. A highly competitive program may be challenging to get into, while a larger or more common one may not. Tuition costs also vary from province to province and there may be some additional fees for out-of-province students, though you may still be eligible for scholarships and Ontario student aid for out-of-province study. If you have the will and the means, it's certainly worth applying and keeping your options open.

Inter-provincial agreements

In some cases, there are agreements crafted between provinces that guarantee a certain number of places to out-of-province students for programs that are not available in their home provinces. If, for example, you are interested in a pharmacy program offered in the French language, which is not offered in Ontario, you may be eligible for one of the few high-demand spots reserved for Ontario students each year at Quebec universities.

If you want to spend a semester or a year or more studying in another province and then transfer your earned credits back to an Ontario college or university, you should start by contacting a transfer specialist at the Ontario school to find out more information and confirm your options. If you plan to complete a program at a school elsewhere in Canada, ensure that the credentials you will earn are from a licensed post-secondary institution and will be recognized anywhere in Canada. You can search for educational institutions across Canada with the Canadian Information Centre for International Credentials' search tool, at https://www.cicic.ca/868/search_the_directory_of_educational_institutions_in_canada.canada).

The website www.UniversityStudy.ca is a good resource to search for programs and links to Canadian universities. In addition, Colleges and Institutes Canada offers links to 139 public colleges across Canada on their website, https://www.collegesinstitutes.ca/our-members/member-directory/.

Being an international student is an amazing way to learn about the way of life in other parts of the world and expand your own outlook and self-efficacy, while also achieving your educational goals. The trick to international study is ensuring beforehand that your credits, diploma or degree earned outside of Canada will be acknowledged when you return home. You

Studying internationally

must apply to foreign post-secondary institutions through the individual schools. Warning: tuition fees required of international students are generally much higher than those paid by domestic students – sometimes three or four times higher. If you qualify for student aid, you may be able to access loans or grants from the Ontario Student Assistance Program for international study, as long as the institution is approved for study by the government of Ontario. You can check whether your prospective school is approved for student loan purposes (or request that its approval be considered) through the links on the Government of Ontario's information site: https://www.ontario.ca/page/study-abroad.

Alternately, many Ontario colleges and universities have partnerships or agreements with academic institutions elsewhere in the world, giving you a different kind of opportunity to study internationally and transfer your credits or qualifications back to Ontario. These student exchanges usually last for one semester to one year. The International Office at your college or university would be the best place to get more information on international study arrangements. And, as mentioned earlier, some universities incorporate international study, internships and field placement opportunities as an option within some of their programs, in which case you might join some of your Canadian classmates in spending a semester or two at a foreign institution – talk to the coordinator of your prospective post-secondary program(s) to see if they offer this option. This route may be less expensive and require less planning on your part.

If you plan to study internationally, you may find more useful information about the benefits, the drawbacks, and the application process through the Canadian Information Centre for International Credentials (https://www.cicic.ca/973/learn_about_the_benefits_of_international_studies.canada).

Distance Education – Online Learning

Online learning became a common option for post-secondary learning thanks to the COVID-19 pandemic. Many college and university courses switched to an online format, which took a variety of forms: synchronous (students and instructors meeting online during scheduled class times); asynchronous (course lectures and resources posted online without any scheduled class times); a combination of synchronous and asynchronous; a blend of online classes and on-campus classes, labs or clinics; or even a flexible option with some students in the classroom on campus while others attended virtually at the same time.

Many post-secondary students chose not to register for online classes of any sort during the pandemic. Some found that this type of instruction did not provide the learning environment they needed, while others felt they didn't have the level of self-regulatory study habits required for success online. Other students did not want to spend time and money on school without also enjoying the on-campus social and extra-curricular atmosphere they expected.

There are some students, however, for whom distance education programs offer an excellent educational opportunity. For example, students who are extremely shy may flourish in the anonymity of some online classes. Those who have physical challenges that make participation in on-campus classes difficult may appreciate not having to travel to school. Students who are extremely busy with work or family life may like the convenience of fitting online courses into their schedules. And many students, particularly those from remote communities, prefer to live cheaply or more comfortably at home while attending distance education programs offered at a faraway institution. *[Benefits of online learning]*

Is distance education an appropriate learning environment for you? You may have experienced online learning in high school during the pandemic, so you have some idea what it might be like. But learning online at the post-secondary level requires a higher level of organization and self-regulatory behaviours in order to achieve success. *[Requirements for online learning]*

First, you must be comfortable with the technology you'll be using. For some students, distance education involves a steep learning curve in the use of e-learning technology before classes even begin. This may include:

- making sure your hardware is functioning properly (computer, webcam, audio and microphone)

- using the internet to attend classes and research information
- downloading any required software, apps or resources
- accessing the Learning Management System (LMS) used by the school to provide course content (these vary by institution, and tutorials are always available)
- using desktop or online tools to complete homework (for example, writing, manipulating graphics, creating spreadsheets or other documents – usually, anything beyond basic knowledge that's required by the course will be explained)
- accepting the proctoring of exams, either through an online proctoring system with your own computer or by attending a physical examination centre, if required.

You need to have plenty of self-control and dedication. Online post-secondary courses require even more self-sufficiency than on-campus courses. No one will be reminding you to do your homework, prepare for class, participate, focus, and meet deadlines. You must have the wherewithal to stick to a schedule, plan ahead, keep your materials organized, and turn off all distractions when you need to work. You really must be determined to do what it takes to succeed – just like when you're on-campus, but even more so.

That said, in order to mitigate any potential shortcomings, you may be able to set up a support system through chat groups with your online classmates to keep each other on track, or with the help of the institution's student support department. Perhaps you can enlist family or friends to give reminders and encouragement when needed. Setting up a support system in advance would be a great example of preparation for the challenges of online learning.

When you register for synchronous online classes, you must also be prepared to maintain good online class habits, showing consideration for your instructors and classmates. For example, you need to be able to get up in the morning in time to get dressed, eat, and arrive in class promptly. Simply rolling over and flicking on your Zoom app, leaving your camera off because you haven't showered and because, well, you're actually still in bed, is not a good indicator of engagement and future success.

If distance education may be a good option for you, take a

look at the OntarioLearn website, at www.OntarioLearn.com. OntarioLearn is a consortium of the province's 24 public colleges that share hundreds of courses leading to either partly- or completely-online certificates and diplomas. Individual colleges frequently have other online full-time and part-time certificate, diploma and micro-credential programs available to students – you can find out more by clicking through the programs on OntarioColleges.ca, or by checking out individual college websites. Another resource for finding distance education college courses and programs is eCampus Ontario (https://learnonline.ecampusontario.ca/).

Other distance education options will be available through Ontario's private career colleges. To find out if a program you're considering is offered online, you'll need to check out each college individually through a career college search, such as the one available at https://www.pcc.tcu.gov.on.ca/PARIS-SearchWeb/search.xhtml.

Many universities have also been offering distance education for decades, frequently in the form of Continuing Education certificates, but online delivery of undergraduate and graduate courses has exploded in recent years. Some degree programs are now offered completely online, for either part-time or full-time study. Most online programs are in the arts, social sciences, and business fields, which do not involve time spent in labs or clinics, although some online science programs are available, such as those at Laurentian and Queens universities. You can search through the listings on the eCampus Ontario website, which has links to the distance education programs and online courses at all 45 colleges and universities in Ontario, at https://learnonline.ecampusontario.ca/.

Of course, when considering distance learning, you are not limited to colleges or universities located in Ontario – you can access distance education options from post-secondary institutions across Canada, and even internationally. For example, Athabasca University in Alberta has specialized in online education since the 1990's. Again, you may be eligible for loans or grants through the Ontario Student Assistance Program for either interprovincial or international learning. Start your research of interprovincial distance education options at

Researching distance education programs

www.UniversityStudy.ca and https://www.collegesinstitutes.ca/our-members/member-directory/. To find international distance education opportunities, search by either post-secondary (or "tertiary") institutions or by the specific programs or topics that interest you, and the country you want to go to, and then study your options carefully.

Questions to ask yourself:

- What post-secondary pathways can lead to the initial career options you're thinking about?

- Is a program that interests you offered at a private or public college, university, or another type of post-secondary institution? Is this type of program available at more than one kind of institution?

- Which type of post-secondary institution offers you the type of educational program that best fits your time, financial and learning needs?

- Is it worthwhile for you to travel outside of Ontario for your post-secondary education? Why is this a better choice?

- Is distance education a good option for you? Do you have the strong self-regulatory behaviours needed to succeed with online learning?

- Have you talked to a school guidance counsellor or post-secondary advisor about your options and have your questions answered?

Narrowing Down Your Preferences

Clearly, the options for post-secondary learning in Ontario can be absolutely overwhelming, particularly for those students who are unsure of the direction they want to take. With an abundance of post-secondary campuses offering thousands of different programs all across Ontario, it can take many months to narrow down the options to a few potential starting points. Once you've begun focusing your potential career interests and feel somewhat ready for post-secondary, your next step is to gather information about the programs and institutions out there, to determine which ones might best meet your needs.

Start your in-depth program and institution research

How to go about this? Research, research, research! Pretty much everything about every program offered by every post-secondary institution in the province is available on the institutions' web pages – some websites are much easier to navigate than others, but they've all got the basic information you'll need, plus contact email addresses and phone numbers to get any answers you can't find yourself. But, as already said, you could spend months surfing through these websites, trying to get an idea of what's out there and looking for... well, something interesting. This would probably be the least efficient and least effective way to start your research.

If you have only a slim idea of initial careers that interest you, or if you have a pretty good idea but haven't yet nailed down the details, there are two better places to start checking out the options:

1 Get hold of program catalogues or "viewbooks" from the Ontario colleges and/or universities by submitting a request or downloading them from their websites. Every program on offer will be described. When you take a gander through these listings, you will probably be astounded by all the amazing programs available in the province, some of which you'd never imagined! With all these catalogues in front of you, it will be very easy to see and compare all the options in your areas of interest.

2 If you've got some ideas already, then you can check out the search engines at OntarioColleges.ca and OntarioUniversitiesInfo.ca to look up information on all the different programs at our public colleges and universities. By searching for "architecture," "computer science" or "media," for instance, you may discover sub-categories that you didn't even know existed... and that may arouse your curiosity.

Choosing what and where to study for one to four years of your life just by surfing the internet will likely feel inadequate. There are other, more personal ways to get an even better feel for the options that are most suitable for you.

If you live in Southern Ontario, it may be possible for you to check out the offerings from most of the universities in the province, all in one place: the Ontario Universities Fair (ontariouniversitiesfair.ca) . Usually held in Toronto in September, this is a huge event where each institution has a booth manned by knowledgeable university staff (often former students) who can answer your questions about available programs, housing, financial aid, student services, etc. The Ontario university information site also maintains a listing of tours and special program events coming up at universities across the province: https://www.ontariouniversitiesinfo.ca/universities/events. In addition, some high schools or communities host an event with a group of university representatives who are eager to give you information, pass out their viewbooks, and answer your questions.

Universities Fair

Ontario colleges, on the other hand, have organized a virtual fair accessible to all interested future students (ontariocollegefair.ca); this event in October, along with the Ontario colleges' Virtual Mondays (ontariocolleges.ca/en/colleges/college-recruitment), provide an opportunity to learn more about the public colleges and meet virtually with advisors and professors. Colleges typically also send representatives to most high schools throughout the province each fall as a way for students to connect with them and ask questions – you may need to sign up for these sessions with your guidance department. Some students start attending them in grade 11.

Colleges virtual fair

Of course, having a million options doesn't always make it easier to make choices. Having done your research, you'll probably have seen that there are many hundreds of programs available to potential students. You may have decided on a couple of possible career directions that sound promising, however you may also have found that a *dozen* different post-secondary institutions are offering *two dozen* similar but slightly different programs related to those career directions. If it looks like you can get where you want to go by following many different routes in many different places, how will you narrow down your options to the ones that would be best for you?

Personal Considerations — Your Needs

Start with you. The first chapters of this book had you thinking about your personal desires and needs, and now you can use that knowledge in crossing some of those options off your list (or finding some to add to your list).

Bear in mind your interests, aptitudes, strengths and values as you sift through all the possibilities you've uncovered. When you have a clear idea of your own desires – the kinds of things you like doing, what you like learning about, the ways you absorb and process information best, where you like being – you can more easily match up those desires with what's on offer out there in the post-secondary world.

As previously discussed, time limitations and financial restraints may greatly affect your post-secondary search. You may not have the option of choosing from everything that's offered in Ontario – your choices may be narrowed down for you by practical considerations. If you are unable to move to another location, for instance, you must consider what is offered at your local institutions. Think about whether you should limit your program and institution search to local facilities, shorter length programs, or online programs that might meet your goals without damaging other areas of your life. *Consider your restraints*

Indigenous students may wish to consider whether your potential post-secondary school offers supports and services specific to your cultural and learning needs. The Ontario Universities website includes a large amount of general information geared toward Indigenous students (https://www.ontariouniversitiesindigenous.ca/). A list of Indigenous student centres and other resources is also available through the Ontario Native Education Counselling Association, at http://oneca.com/transitions/colleges-and-universities.html. *Indigenous student resources*

Many students also have distinct physical, mental health and/or learning needs that must be met in order to achieve success in their post-secondary education. All public universities and colleges in Ontario are obligated to remove systemic barriers to students' education. Physical and mental health accommodations may be available but not be obvious, so you may need to enquire about having these needs met. Academic accommo- *Physical, mental health and academic accommodations*

dations are changes to the learning environment that give students equal access to learning (like an Individual Education Plan, or IEP, in high school); accommodations are made available to students on an individual basis, and in confidentiality.

Student accessibility services offices (a.k.a. "student services" or "student success") are extremely helpful. Be sure to notify them early on if you've had an IEP in high school and wish to continue the accommodations – you may need updated testing, and that takes time to organize. As well, if you qualify for OSAP funding, you will be eligible for a subsidy for any necessary technology. The accessibility office will request copies of your IPRC statement of decision, your most recent IEP, and your last psychoeducational assessment report, so be sure to get this paperwork from your high school.

An online transition resource guide for students with disabilities provides some information for students considering or attending post-secondary institutions in Ontario (https://www.transitionresourceguide.ca/blog/high-school-post-secondary). If the availability and quality of accommodations are a significant factor in your program and institution search, you can check out the accessibility resources available at each Ontario university (https://www.ontariouniversitiesinfo.ca/accessibility) and public college (https://osca.ca/ontario-college-accessibility-and-disability-services/). You might feel more confident in your choices, however, if you take the time to talk about your needs with experts at the student services (or "student success" or "accommodations") offices at the schools you are considering, particularly if you are interested in a private career college or in studying outside of Ontario. Depending on your personal situation, you may also need to pay special attention to other factors, such as your housing and transportation needs, or the availability of assistive software, when choosing your post-secondary path.

And, again, connect to your values! Do the programs you're looking at match your core values in some way that will bring you satisfaction? If you love adventure, for instance, prioritize programs that involve travel, the outdoors, or exploration of some sort. If you value leadership, you may be interested in a business, education or political program. Your values can be

Consider your values

met in indirect ways, however. If helping others is one of your core values, you'll probably want to look for a career where you will fulfill that desire, but this doesn't necessarily mean a client-centred career – medical research, educational administration or non-fiction publishing could also meet this core value. Think outside the box!

Another example: according to an American study, those who earn a diploma are likely to earn, on average, *one million dollars more* during their work life than those who do not.[13] Many people value the comfort that comes with a certain level of income in their lifestyle, and this motivates their choices when it comes to a career. In this case, consulting data about employment rates and incomes of post-secondary graduates may help in choosing a career direction (review the labour market tools in the "What Are You Aiming For" section in Chapter 2, as well as "Institution Considerations," coming up).

Post-secondary education is an expensive investment, so think clearly about *what* you want to do and *where* you want to be. You do not need to plan too far into the future (most students can't do that at this point anyway), but you do need to take a first step that *makes sense for you*.

Questions to ask yourself:

- Do you have any personal desires or needs related to the location, costs, housing availability or quality of life of your future post-secondary institution? What are they?

- Do you have physical, mental health or learning needs that may require accommodation? If so, have you confirmed what is available for you at any school that you may be considering? Do you have your documents in order?

Program Considerations

Now, get out your pencil and paper, or open a spreadsheet file on your computer to keep track of all the information you find. You may end up with many more potential programs and pathways than you expected! On the other hand, you may find that you're not as qualified as you thought, or that there as not as many suitable options as you assumed. Either way, the choices you eventually make on your post-secondary applications will come much more easily if you take the time to record and organize the data you find on the programs and schools that catch your interest (the courses, prerequisites, tuition fees, residences, extra-curricular opportunities, etc.) as you go along.

Start Your Research

Compile data about potential programs

If you have any idea of the career direction(s) you're aiming for, you can start narrowing down your program choices by researching more specific details about related programs that each institution offers. As suggested previously, use OntarioColleges.ca and/or OntarioUniversitiesInfo.ca to search for schools that offer specific programs, or, alternately, to look through all the programs offered by specific schools. You can then follow through to more detailed information by clicking on links to the programs' and/or schools' own websites. Use fairly broad search terms related to your career direction in order to bring up all the possibilities – as mentioned previously, you may discover programs that are in some ways similar to what you were thinking about, yet different enough to take you on a detour that you hadn't yet considered.

Alternately, cozy up with those college and university catalogues you requested from the institutions, collected at a college or university fair, or downloaded to your computer. Highlight anything that sounds interesting and then get the program details from the schools' websites.

Of course, if you make a simple online request, any post-secondary institution will be more than happy to send you an information package in the mail, or to answer your questions by phone or email. They will all want to recruit you!

Dive deep into the details!

As you zero in on the programs that appeal to you, it's important to carefully read through every bit of information you can find about them, in order to have a clear understanding of what is involved in these programs, what their expected outcomes will be, and whether they will fit your needs. Once you've found programs that sound particularly promising to you, follow through in three levels of depth to get an idea of what each program would involve:

1. First, check out each program's website. For example, if you're interested in a college program in hospitality or tourism management, you'll see on OntarioColleges.ca that there are several colleges with a number of similar or related programs. Click the links to each college's program website, and read through all the information there.

2. Next, explore a little deeper: read through the list of courses you would take to complete their program. Depending on the kind of program you're interested in, the required courses might sound very similar from one institution to another, or might vary quite a bit. You're not likely to be charmed by every course you'll have to take, but if at least half of them sound interesting or worthwhile, then keep going.

3. Dive right down to the footings, and find out what your day-to-day learning might be like as a student in that program. Find the syllabus or course outline for each of those courses – the links may be right there for you to click on, or you may have to search for them on the institution's website. The course outlines will give you a better idea of what you'll actually be studying if you decide to take that program. Don't be intimidated by what you read – you are not expected to understand everything that the course outlines are telling you since you haven't even begun the first step of your learning process yet, but you will get some idea of what that future learning would look like.

Alternate Pathways

Sometimes your career goals can be achieved through more than one route, either through pathways already put in place by post-secondary institutions or by do-it-yourself planning. For example, a career in paramedicine can start with either an intensive 12-month program at a private college or a regular 4-semester program at a public college – they have the same end result, but one route might suit your situation better than the other.

There may also be pathway options that lead to the same general goal, but with a somewhat different end result. A career in nursing, for instance, can be achieved by earning a Bachelor of Science degree in Nursing from a university, or by earning a college diploma in Practical Nursing. These two routes have different requirements for acceptance into their programs, and then have different ranges of responsibility and levels of earning when working as a nurse. That said, it is also not uncommon for Practical Nurses to later take advantage of "bridging" programs between some colleges and universities and return to school to earn a nursing degree (see below).

Likewise, a goal to become, say, an astronomer or a biotechnologist or a physician can be achieved through various direct and indirect routes. Exploring those program websites or searching for further suggestions through career-specific webpages or online chats may be helpful in broadening your options and pathways to your goal. Some professional associations are also valuable sources of information about specific careers (for example, the Ontario Society for Professional Engineers, or the Ontario Dental Hygienists' Association); these organizations are often keen to support future practitioners and willing to inform you of the reality of their professions and the processes to achieve them. Talking to someone in your community (or elsewhere) who is working in your future field of work is also an excellent idea, providing you with valuable insight from their experience, and potentially acting as a mentor over a longer term.

Get personal insight from someone in that field

Choosing a program at one institution may sometimes give you an immediate (or future) association with a second institution, as colleges and universities multiply their campuses and develop multi-institutional connections. Many colleges and universities have articulation agreements, too, which means they offer collaborative programs that combine classes from *both* schools, encompassing the conceptual learning of the university degree and the practical hands-on learning of the college diploma – you will earn both credentials at graduation. This

Collaborative programs between two schools

type of dual experience may be particularly beneficial when starting your career, as you may viewed as needing less training than other graduates when newly employed. Employers love hiring students who have both the practical, hands-on diploma from college and the theoretically-based university degree.

Additionally, many colleges and universities have **advanced transfer** and **bridging** agreements. If you've already earned some post-secondary credits, a new college or university program might accept one or more of those previous courses as advanced transfer credits, so you don't have to re-do them. A bridging process, on the other hand, allows students who have already earned a college diploma to have advanced standing in the university degree program for a related discipline. Sometimes students who do not have certain credits or high enough high school grades for acceptance into a university degree program find they are able to be accepted into college, then transfer or bridge into the upper years of their preferred university program two or three years later. Many such agreements between colleges and universities exist in health care, information technology, science and engineering programs, for example, though their requirements can vary.

Advanced transfers and bridging agreements

You can find a list of the various types of collaborative and associative programs in between Ontario universities and colleges at https://www.ouac.on.ca/guide/collaborative-university-college-programs/.

Your Eligibility

All these available options are great, as long as you can actually get accepted into the ones you want.

Are you eligible for the programs that look interesting to you? Your likelihood of being accepted into a program will depend on your eligibility, and your eligibility depends very highly on your high school grades, so determine if you meet the prerequisites for acceptance into each of the programs you're looking at. What high school courses you've taken is really important (which is why it's best to start thinking about your post-secondary education long before high school graduation). Have you taken all the required high school courses, at the expected levels (i.e., U, M or C), for your preferred programs? Universities require ENG4U and U-level high school courses; some M courses may also be accepted. You can get into college with U, M or C courses.

Program prerequisites In either case, your application will only be considered if you have taken all the prerequisite courses for that program (or acceptable alternates). For example, a Biotechnology *degree* program may require you to have completed six U- or M-level courses, including two U-level sciences, Advanced Functions, and U-level English, and may also recommend that you take Calculus in order to do well in the program. On the other hand, a Biotechnology Technician *diploma* program may require grade 12 U or C-level English, grade 11 U- or C-level Math, and one grade 12 U- or C-level Science. If you don't have the required courses in your background, either from high school or credits from another post-secondary program, you will not even be considered for the program.

Grade requirements And think about the grades you've earned. All university programs and many college programs have specific grade requirements. The schools' individual program websites (and also OntarioColleges.ca or OntarioUniversitiesInfo.ca) may list any *minimum* high school grades required, but even that does not guarantee you'll be accepted, especially if you're applying to a highly competitive program. Many show a "grade range" for admission, which is not a cut-off, just an estimated baseline according to the previous year's applications – it may turn out to be a bit higher or lower this year, so if you're not quite there, you can always go ahead and apply anyway and keep your fingers crossed. If you're a mature student who has been out of high school for a while, these minimum grades will give you an idea of the program's expectations regarding its incoming students, although your work and life experience, as well as any upgrading you've done, may be considered. (See the "Applications" section in Chapter 5 if you want to know more about applications for those not currently in high school.)

How a post-secondary institution calculates your average is up to the institution itself, and may even vary depending on the program. They might calculate your average using all your high school courses, or using just the ones that are prerequisites for the specific program. Typically, your top six 4U or 4M courses are used in the calculation. If you have experienced difficulty in maintaining your previous high school average due to life challenges such as the death of a parent, a major illness, etc., a post-secondary institution with a "special circumstances" admission policy will take this into consideration – talk to your high school guidance counsellor or contact the institution itself for more information.

Calculating your average

There may be additional requirements that affect your likelihood of acceptance into a certain program. Many art-based degree programs will involve an audition or will expect you to submit a portfolio of your work, which may be very simple and general, or may have very detailed and specific submission requirements. Certain programs may request reference letters, and a few programs may consider other experiences, like work or extracurricular activities, as part of their application process. Carefully check all the details of each program's admission requirements.

Auditions, portfolios and references

As suggested previously, keep track of all this information about any programs that have drawn your attention. When it comes time to fill out your applications, being able to easily compare the benefits and drawbacks of each option will make appropriate choices easier to distinguish. If you cross certain programs off your list, don't delete them entirely – noting what it was that put them out of the running may prove helpful later, reminding you of what to watch out for in other programs. Lots of information, all pulled together in some kind of readable format, is what you're aiming for.

Parents' Note:
If your child does not have top grades in high school yet shows interest in a university program with high entrance requirements, you might want to suggest checking out any similar college programs. Look also for any available advanced transfer or bridging agreements between a college and university. This can prove to be a great backup plan! Though colleges frequently have lower grade requirements for acceptance, a college diploma can often be used later for

acceptance and advanced credit in a related university program. The advanced transfer or bridging route usually takes a year or two longer to ultimately reach the desired university degree, but it can be a very effective route if that degree program is your child's ultimate goal.

Questions to ask yourself:

- Have you fully researched all the programs that sound interesting to you? Have you located a list of courses you would need to complete, and found out what those courses would be like?

- Is there more than one pathway to achieve your goal?

- Will you meet the eligibility requirements for the programs you're interested in? Will your current marks earn you admission, or will you need to upgrade your learning in order to be admitted?

- If your marks are not adequate, will you choose a different path to this goal, or will you change your goal?

Institution Considerations

It is very common to be able to narrow down your *program* choices but still be unable to settle on the schools that would be *the best fit for you*. The location and size of the school are very important as well. Would you prefer the anonymity of a big school or the community atmosphere of a small school? Do you plan to live on or near campus? Do you want to play sports, or are you looking for certain social or cultural groups to get involved in? Choosing schools is a big decision... but it's still only a hopeful and well-researched choice of direction that you're making and not necessarily a locked-in, long-term commitment. Your application can include *several* choices, not just one.

First Impressions

What is the likely outcome if you graduate from a specific college or university? Some institutions have a great reputation that attracts students, but this doesn't necessarily mean they'll offer you the career results or even the overall experience that *you* might want from your time there.

If you like statistics, you might be interested in checking out each Ontario college's "key performance indicators" on the Ontario government site https://www.ontario.ca/page/college-graduation-satisfaction-and-job-rates. The stats on each college's graduate satisfaction and employment rates, as well as employers' satisfaction with the graduates they've hired, might help you compare different colleges. Many Ontario universities publish their own data about student satisfaction and post-graduate employment rates on their websites, and some information about university graduation and job rates can also be found at https://www.ontario.ca/page/university-programs-graduation-and-job-rates.

School stats

The best way to get accurate impressions of the schools that interest you? Visiting any promising schools in person is probably the most reliable method of getting to know an institution and what it has to offer, if you have the means. And the best time to start touring your potential school choices is before you start grade 12 – before you have to actually start narrowing down your preferences and making decisions. In addition to offering general tours for interested students year-round, most schools organize open houses once or twice a year (once in the spring, at least, and often during March break). Attending an open house is a great way to get your questions answered, see the campus (classrooms, labs, public areas, residences, food outlets, athletic centres, etc.), get a better understanding of its location, and get a feel for the atmosphere of the place. It's easier to sense the vibe of the institution and feel whether or not you can see yourself there if you visit the place in person, and it also makes going away to school less scary. You may be able to meet with coordinators or instructors for your potential program, or even current students, to get more details about what it's like. If personal meetings are not an option during the open

Visit the school

house, you might set up an appointment to meet with a program advisor, liaison or coordinator at another time. Most colleges and universities also present virtual open houses and virtual meetings with program advisors, which can be a useful substitute if traveling to campus is not possible.

Living Arrangements

In addition to the programs offered at various schools, you may have other things to think about when narrowing down your options. For instance, if you don't intend to continue living at home while going to school, how far away are you willing to travel? Where will you live? In this case, your housing options will be of great importance.

Residences — Residence accommodations generally provide an excellent first step for young students moving away from home for the first time. Often, acceptance into residence is guaranteed for first-year students who apply by the deadline and are accepted into a program. Residence costs may be somewhat higher than off-campus housing, but you won't be required to sign a full year's lease or buy any furniture, you'll be conveniently and safely close to your classes and other school facilities, you'll have the support of residence staff and mentors 24/7, and you'll often have the simplicity of an available meal plan. Residences may offer single rooms, double rooms, multi-person dorms, suite-style mini-apartments, or townhouses, with mandatory or optional meal plans of varying styles and costs. Study both the room plans and food plans carefully, as each has pros and cons. You may also find that some schools have no residences with room styles that are acceptable to you, or may not offer any meal plans, or may have residences that are some distance from the campus location. If you want to live in residence, be sure you know what each of your potential schools offers.

Off-campus housing — If you plan to live off-campus but don't already have connections to the area around a potential new school, your task will be a bit trickier. If you can, get to know the areas near campus where you might find acceptable and affordable housing. Many schools maintain off-campus housing directories, so look for that on their websites, and check out the current offerings on sites like kijiji.ca and rentals.ca to see what the rental market looks like in that area. What's available will change depending on the time of year, but you might get a general idea of prices and types of housing options nearby. Aside from apartments, students often find affordable rooms or basement apartments in private homes, or individual rooms in student-leased houses and townhouses. The off-campus housing market can be very competitive, and sometimes there are dozens of applications for a unit. Be sure to apply quickly if you find a space you like, and have references ready.

Access to transportation, grocery stores and other amenities is important to consider as well. Many post-secondary institutions provide a student pass for public transportation with their ancillary fees (though you can sometimes opt out of this and get a refund if you don't need it).

The availability and affordability of housing is an important factor that can strike a post-secondary institution off your list. You will find further discussion of residence and off-campus housing in the "Living Arrangements" section of Chapter 5.

Extracurriculars

Finally, what about your non-academic life? Classes are only part of the experience of a post-secondary education! The social connections you will make, and the clubs, sports, arts and other activities you anticipate enjoying are also extremely important. What extra-curricular opportunities does each institution offer? Search the schools' websites for student groups related to specific programs or faculties, recreational sports and facilities, school teams, residence activities, and student-run clubs and events (often found under "student life" or "student council," or something similar). Getting involved in extra-curricular activities – joining a club, playing an intramural sport, etc. – is an important avenue for meeting new people and enjoying post-secondary life to the fullest.

The notable information you find about each post-secondary institution you're considering can be added to your information spreadsheet. After all, combining the results from your program research and these notes on each institution will make a pros and cons list easier to produce when you're ready to make some choices.

Questions to ask yourself:

- Which of the schools that offer programs leading to your chosen career(s) also meet your personal needs and desires?
- Are you able to visit any schools that interest you? If not, will you participate in virtual open houses or other events? Are you prepared to seek answers to any questions you might still have about a school and/or its program?
- Does a school that you're considering provide residence housing and a meal plan that suits you?
- Is there appropriate and reasonable off-campus housing available near a school that interests you?
- Do your preferred schools offer extracurricular facilities and activities that appeal to you?

Making Final Choices

Actually, there are no final choices. There are final decisions on what to put on your post-secondary application forms before the submission deadline, but those can be changed if need be. And even after starting your post-secondary education, changes can certainly still be made – you are not signing away your whole future!

So you've trimmed down your list of possibilities. You've got some ideas about career directions that interest you, and you've found a number of post-secondary institutions with programs related to them. How do you know which are the best programs at the best institutions for you to apply to? And then, if you end up receiving several offers of admission, how will you choose which one to accept?

Once you've narrowed down where you *can* go, you just need to consider where you *want* to go. This is when you'll compare all the details and impressions you gleaned from your research: the details you found about each program's costs and the courses you would take there, each school's location and residence and extra-curricular offerings, and any other information you heard or read about. If, as suggested, you have compiled this information as you found it, it will now be easy to assess the benefits and drawbacks of each program and school. So *do* actually assess them – think carefully about everything you know about these programs and schools, and consider how they will meet your needs en route to your goals.

Having all the data together in one spot will help you rank the post-secondary options that you've still got on your list – some sort of ranking is what you will want when you begin your applications. Things can still change, of course. No decision has to be permanent – there's still time to find additional information that might make you change your mind – but being as well-informed and prepared as possible when beginning your application will make the months that follow much less stressful.

Questions to ask yourself:

- What programs appeal to you the most? Why?
- Which schools appeal to you the most? Why?

5

HOW TO GET WHERE YOU'RE GOING
(Doing the "paperwork")

Applications

When you've made a decision to apply for a certificate, diploma and/or degree (or all three), you've accomplished the first big step in launching toward your initial career direction. Now comes what some people would consider the hard part: filling out applications, and... waiting. Let the countdown begin!

If you are now in your last year of high school, you will probably be having group or individual meetings with a school guidance counsellor to walk you through the process of applying for post-secondary education. Be sure to take notes at these sessions, as there will be a large amount of information and many new terms coming at you quickly. No matter which post-secondary option you've chosen – private career college, public college or university, or distance education – there will be online application forms with deadlines for submission. This is the perfect opportunity for you to develop and practice some soft skills that you will use throughout your life: researching and attending to the process, dealing with paperwork, considering your needs and how to get help or answers, and communicating with strangers. Taking charge and being responsible for working through the application process will build your self-efficacy.

If you plan to attend college or university part-time, you may need to follow a somewhat different application process, which varies by institution. Contact the individual college or university for their specific information on applying for part-time studies.

Parents' Note:
Your child's secondary school may post updates on their website or have an information night for parents to learn about the process of applying for post-secondary education. The process may feel confusing or intimidating for a young person, so the more you know about it yourself, the better you'll be able to help with the "paperwork" and reassure your child about the progress of their applications.

It's also a great idea to spend your waiting time making further enquiries about the programs and universities you've applied for. University open houses and virtual tours take place throughout the spring, and this is a great time to arrange for a visit to campus with a private tour of the department(s) to which you've applied, if you haven't already. If you're able to talk to students in those departments, ask them about their experiences within the program, including their opinions about any pros and the cons. Making connections like this may help you pin down your preferences from among the schools you applied to.

Parents' Note:
Your child's post-secondary application(s) may ask for a second contact person to be informed of all essential communications, or to act as a backup in case your child can't be reached. Your child can choose to opt in or out of this arrangement. If they agree to it, confirm that your contact information has been added correctly.

University Applications

The Ontario Universities Application Centre (OUAC) website (https://www.ouac.on.ca/) has lots of information about the university application process, the information required, deadlines, application fees, links to the universities, and an extensive Frequently Asked Questions section. It is the portal used to apply for all Ontario universities. OUAC provides application guides for those still in high school who will apply with the Un-

Ontario Universities Application Centre

dergrad 101 application form (https://www.ouac.on.ca/guide/101-guide/), and for those who are not currently in high school who will use the Undergrad 105 application form (https://www.ouac.on.ca/guide/105-guide/).

If you are currently in high school (including those doing a victory lap) and will earn your high school diploma this year, your university applications will begin with logging onto the OUAC account created by your school. The school will inform you of your school number, access number, and PIN, usually in November. Save these numbers, and use them to access your account and the OUAC 101 application form on the OUAC website. Most schools will automatically upload your grade 11 grades and your grade 12 midterm and final grades to the OUAC site, however you would be wise to check that your marks are listed correctly and there are no omissions on your application. Marks from e-learning, summer school or Virtual High School courses are easily lost, so check your electronic transcript carefully.

In 2022, it will cost $150 for you to apply to *up to three programs* (whether they're all at the same university or at three different universities); you can easily apply to more than three programs, and will simply be charged an extra $50 for each additional choice. A few university programs have supplemental application fees as well. Payment can be made with a credit card or through online banking with some banks (which takes several days to process, so don't wait until just before the deadline). It's important to note that you are only allowed to apply to a *maximum of three different programs at any one university*, although you can change your program choices without any charge before the programs' deadlines.

Since your application fee includes three programs, be sure to apply to at least three programs. Even if you already know the one that you really, really want, it's always a good idea to have a plan B and C. It happens on occasion that a program is cancelled or modified due to unforeseen circumstances; it also happens that students are unexpectedly denied an offer of admission for various reasons.

Each specific program at each university has its own OUAC code to be used on your application.

The deadline to submit your OUAC 101 application is usually mid-January – you can find the exact date here: https://www.ouac.on.ca/deadlines/. This deadline is called the "equal consideration date": when you submit by this date, your application will be considered for acceptance along with everyone who has submitted up until that date (ie, it won't be "first come, first served" until after that date). You may submit an application later, of course, however you are not guaranteed equal consideration for acceptance if you apply late, and you will likely be too late for acceptance into any highly competitive programs. There are also a number of universities that accept students into various programs with classes that start in January or May (https://www.ouac.on.ca/guide/101-winter-admission/ #winter).

Mid-January "equal consideration" deadline

If you apply to more than one university, you can rank your university preferences in any order – in *most* cases, it does not make a difference to your acceptance status at any of them. However, if you apply for more than one *program* at one university, you should rank these programs in order of your preference. If you are offered admission to one of the programs, the university may choose not to offer you admission to any program that you ranked lower, because they naturally assume you are less interested in lower-ranked programs. You can change your rankings with no charge at any time, even after having received an offer of admission, by accessing your online application. Remember, though, that some programs are in high demand and will not accept new applications beyond their stated deadlines.

Ranking programs

All the universities you have applied to will confirm that your application has been received, and will probably send you an information package in the mail. Some programs require supplementary application documents, such as a portfolio, or require auditions or interviews. These requirements are available in the program's admissions information web page, and you will receive further details when you apply to the program. These must be submitted or completed by the university's stated deadline in order for you to continue to be considered for admission.

Supplementary application documents

You may also apply for residence on your university applications, if you wish.

If you wish to study part-time, taking three or fewer courses

[margin note: Part-time studies]

per semester, the application procedure may vary depending on the university – some may require you to apply with the OUAC 105 online form, while others may want you to apply directly to the university. Check your potential universities' websites for up-to-date information about part-time applications.

University Applicants Not Currently in Secondary School

The university application process for non-high school students is similar to that above, but with a few important differences. If you have been out of school for more than seven months, you are 21 years of age or older, or you have previously attended a post-secondary institution, you will go through a slightly different channel on the OUAC website. Extensive information is available on the OUAC site, at https://www.ouac.on.ca/ouac-105/.

After you create your OUAC account, use the OUAC 105 application form to apply to an Ontario university. The form becomes available in September for the following year, and you may submit only one application per school year. You will receive a reference number when your application is complete.

[margin note: OUAC 105]

It's important to save this reference number, as you may need it in the future if you apply for post-graduate studies such as physiotherapy, medical school, or a Masters program. The deadline for your application will depend on the program you're applying for: the general deadlines for Law, Education and Rehabilitation Sciences are listed at https://www.ouac.on.ca/deadlines/; for other programs, check your institution's website or click the links on the OUAC 105 site.

The fees for your OUAC 105 application are slightly higher than those for the OUAC 101: currently, $156 for your three base program choices, plus $50 for each additional choice.

[margin note: $156 for 3 programs ($50 per additional)]

There may also be a supplemental document evaluation fee that varies by university; fees to request transcripts from any previously attended post-secondary institutions, if necessary; and possibly the supplemental program fees required by a few specific programs.

University Offers of Admission

Offers of admission will be sent to you, with details and instructions, from the universities themselves – the universities make their admission decisions, not the OUAC. Your offers will also be viewable on the OUAC website. Offers may come with conditions, such as maintaining a certain grade average on your final grades, in order to be finalized; your offer may be revoked if you do not maintain your marks. If you have not been accepted into a program you applied to, you may be offered admission to another somewhat similar program at that university. If you applied by the January deadline, you should receive any offers of admission by the end of May. Your acceptance offer will indicate the deadline for you to accept the offer, the deposit required, any entrance scholarships you qualify for, as well as a room if you applied for residence. If you have questions about the status of your application or an offer you've received, get answers by contacting the university directly.

Offers presented by the end of May

You typically have until June 1 to accept your offers on the OUAC website, though some programs may state a later deadline in their offer of acceptance (particularly if you've been granted late admission into a program). Accepting a university's offer will probably also require the payment of a registration deposit within a specified amount of time. To accept (or decline) an offer, you must access your OUAC account and select "accept" (or "decline") for the offers available; you must then "submit" and also "verify" your choices. You will be given a confirmation number, so keep this for your records – glitches have been known to happen. Once these changes have been processed (which may take a few days), your new status will be available on the OUAC site and you will receive further communications from your chosen university.

Registration deposit for the offer you accept

You do not need to accept or decline any offers until their stated deadline – though of course you can, if you're sure about what you want. You may want to give yourself time to see all your options before making a final decision, although accepting one offer does not affect your applications to other universities. And, if you change your mind, you can also cancel your acceptance of an offer of admission and accept a different one that's still available (if you receive a late offer, for example) through the same process on the OUAC site.

You can change your mind until your acceptance deadline!

Your ability to defer an accepted offer of admission to the next semester or next year depends on the program and the university. Contact the university admissions office for information on that.

Finally, if you missed the application deadline, it does not necessarily mean that the program you're interested in is already full. Likewise, if you did not receive an offer of admission after applying, it does not necessarily mean you're too late to get into a different program. Some programs will still accept new students right up until September, if they have space available; some highly competitive programs carry a wait list, so an offer could come late. Starting in early June, the OUAC Admissions Information Service will open a searchable database, so you can browse to see what programs are still open and accepting students: https://www.ouac.on.ca/apply/referral/en_CA/referral/index.

Late offers of admission

College Applications

Much like the Ontario Universities Application Centre, those planning to attend college have a one-stop shop for information and applications: www.OntarioColleges.ca. Here you will be able to research the many programs available at Ontario's 24 colleges and link to the individual college's websites to find more details about their program lengths, programs locations (if they have more than one campus location) tuition costs, admission requirements, residence information, etc.

Ontario Colleges Application Service

You can apply for college in Ontario by creating an account with the Ontario Colleges Application Service (OCAS), accessible directly from the OntarioColleges.ca website (https://www.ontariocolleges.ca/en/apply-now) or by downloading the app to your phone. The online application service opens in October for college programs that will start in the fall of the following year. There is a non-refundable fee, currently $95.00, which allows you to apply to *up to five* different programs, with a *maximum of three programs at any one college*.

$95 for 5 programs

Take advantage of the opportunity to apply to multiple programs with the single application fee. It is always recommended to have a backup plan, in case there are program changes or you don't receive the offer of admission that you were anticipating.

February 1st is the deadline for applications if you wish to be considered equally with all other applicants for a spot in your preferred programs. You may choose to apply later as some programs will continue to accept applications until September, but most highly competitive programs will be considered full after February 1st. Many other popular programs will maintain waitlists through the spring and summer, until they are confirmed full. You can search for programs that remain open and accepting students here: https://www.ontariocolleges.ca/en/programs. If you wish, you can also make changes to the programs you've already chosen by accessing your application after the deadline. *[Feb. 1 "equal consideration" deadline]*

Most high schools will upload midterm and final marks of their current students to the site automatically, though it is recommended that you check to ensure they are listed correctly on your application.

Collaborative, advanced transfer and bridging programs were described in the section What Post-Secondary Options are Available. *Most* collaborative programs that are completed through both a college and a university require you to apply through the university (ie, through OUAC – see the University Applications section above). Advanced transfer and bridging programs, however, require you to apply through the college.

Depending on the program(s) you've applied to, you may be required to undergo testing (such as a language proficiency test, or the Health Occupations Aptitude Exam (HOAE) for entrance to some health programs) or to submit other supporting documents to OntarioColleges.ca or to the college directly. Check with the college(s) for any specific instructions if this is the case for your chosen program(s). *[Additional documents]*

College Applicants Not Currently in Secondary School

If you are not a high school student, you are among the majority of applicants to Ontario's colleges. You, too, must apply to your chosen programs through OntarioColleges.ca and adhere to the requirements and deadlines above, but as your situation may be a little bit more complicated, it's possible that your admission process will be a little bit more complicated as well.

Request an official high school or college transcript, or GED result

Non-high school students will need to request a transcript of their high school grades to submit to OntarioColleges.ca. Most Ontario high schools will submit electronic transcripts directly to OCAS for a fee that's payable with your college application – there will be a check box on your OCAS application if this is an option for you. Otherwise, you will need to request that your former high school mail a sealed official paper transcript to OntarioColleges.ca (only a sealed official transcript will be accepted).

Mature students (those over 19 who do not have a high school diploma) can apply to college through OntarioColleges.ca, but should contact their future college(s) to confirm their entrance requirements. If you passed a GED test, ask the institution that tested you to send your official results. In addition, if you have previously registered in a public or private college, including for academic upgrading, you must provide a transcript of your college grades when applying to a *new* college – these can also be submitted electronically as part of your application (with the specified fee) if coming from a public college. Transcripts from private career colleges may be available online through https://careercollegesontario.ca/transcripts/; other private colleges must be individually asked to mail official transcripts to OntarioColleges.ca.

Prior Learning Assessment

Some people plan to attend college to upgrade or retrain after already having undertaken non-traditional forms of learning, or having relevant non-academic work or life experience. Many Ontario colleges have a Prior Learning Assessment and Recognition (PLAR) process that may be used to evaluate potential students' current knowledge and skills and, if applicable, offer admission or even advanced credits (including language credits) in a post-secondary program. Individual colleges should be contacted to find out if a PLAR assessment might be appropriate for your situation.

College Offers of Admission

Ontario colleges may start sending out offers of admission as of February 1st, however applicants have until May 1st to confirm their acceptance of an offer of admission. Programs that continue to have open spots will still accept new applications and send offers of admission until the beginning of the semester; if you receive a late offer of admission, be careful to check for the deadline to accept it. *[Most offers must be accepted by May 1]*

Accepting an offer of admission is easily done through your dashboard on your OntarioColleges.ca account, and the other colleges will be notified. If you later change your mind or receive a more desirable offer, you can change your acceptance on your dashboard to any offer that has not yet expired. Only one offer acceptance can be submitted per day. It is not necessary to physically decline any offers that you don't want to pursue.

All colleges will require a tuition deposit be paid by mid-June (or later for late admissions); the amount varies by college, but is often between $250-$500. Check your offer of admission to verify the deposit amount and the deadline for payment. This tuition deposit confirms your intention to register, so if you don't pay it you may forfeit your spot in the program. *[Tuition deposit]*

Royal Military College Applications

RMC may accept high school graduates with final grades above 75% in English, math and other required subjects, or mature students (those 21 years of age or older applying to programs other than science and engineering, without the prerequisites) to the Regular Officer Training Program (ROTP). Information on the required application process for those from

Apply via the Armed Forces

a variety of different circumstances is available on their website, https://www.rmc-cmr.ca/en/registrars-office/rmc-admissions. Your application to RMC must be started by applying to the Canadian Armed Forces, at https://forces.ca/en/apply-now/.

Private College Applications

Private career colleges, Indigenous Institutes and Bible colleges have varying start dates for their programs, so their admission requirements and application deadlines will also vary. Contact these post-secondary institutions directly to get more information on their programs, individual application processes, fees, accommodations, etc. (See "Private Colleges" in Chapter 4.)

Inter-Provincial and International Applications

To apply to a Canadian university or college outside of Ontario, you will need to search for the application and admission information for Canadian students on the institution's website, to ensure that you meet all the necessary requirements for acceptance. If the names of courses, course levels, programs, etc., is a bit confusing because it differs from those in Ontario, send a message or call the school to get clarification. You will likely need to submit your application directly to the post-secondary institution.

Apply directly

If you want to study outside of Canada in a program that is not offered in conjunction with an Ontario college or university, you must apply to your intended international program by contacting the institution itself. Be careful to get all the details about program length and start date, application requirements and deadlines, and any other information they might be able to provide (e.g. visa requirements, accommodations, international student organizations, work permits, etc.) beforehand. Also, be prepared to pay higher tuition fees, as institutions typically charge more to international students. (See "Inter-Provincial and International Options" in Chapter 4.)

Not Accepted (When No Offer is Forthcoming)

Here's a hard truth: not everyone gets accepted into their first-choice program on their first try. In fact, many don't. But if you don't get accepted, it does not mean that all hope is lost. Time, experience and an open mind can still set you on a satisfactory career path – perhaps the one you had originally hoped for, or perhaps a somewhat different one.

You may have your heart set on a particular program at a particular school, but if it's a competitive program and your application doesn't quite meet the level required to put you on the list – whether those requirements include the highest grades, or specific high school credits, or a top-notch portfolio, or certain previous experiences – you just might not make the cut. Maybe you'll be surprised, or maybe you won't.

In some cases, when a school cannot offer you admission to the program you applied to, they may instead offer admission to an alternate program that is similar or somehow related. If you wish, you can choose to accept this alternate offer because it sounds like an interesting option for you. You can also choose to accept the offer because it provides a route for you to take post-secondary courses that might help you *transfer back* into your preferred program in the future. To explore any options that this different offer will provide, you should talk to an admissions officer or academic advising counsellor at the school in question. *Alternate offers of admission*

In a similar vein, if you don't get accepted into a specific program that you wanted, you could try to gain acceptance into a more general program at that school by changing or adding to your college or university application. By spending a semester or a year in a general program, you can take some of the courses that will be of use to you if you re-apply to *transfer* into your preferred program later. As an example, say you were not accepted into astrophysics or biomedical engineering; by enrolling in a *general* science or engineering program, you should be able to take some of the courses you would have been taking in first-year astrophysics or biomedical engineering, so there will be little course catch-up to do if you are able to re-apply and transfer into astrophysics or biomedical engineering the following year. In this scenario, you may need some help figuring out which courses you can and should register for in that first year, which could include the elective courses required during the preferred program.

Other options — On the other hand, perhaps you'll choose to see a lack of offers as a sign that you're meant to explore other options – a gap year, or a different kind of educational program altogether. Switching gears and taking time to work, travel or seek out new options could end up being even more satisfying and enlightening than your original plans would have been.

Of course, if you've done your homework before completing your post-secondary applications, there shouldn't be too many surprises when the offers roll in... or don't, as the case may be. You'll already know how competitive the programs are, what their admission requirements are, and what their grade cut-off ranges are likely to be. You'll have an idea of what your chance of acceptance is. And you'll already have integrated Plans B and C into your multiple program applications, because you didn't want to count your chickens before they were hatched... Right?

Questions to ask yourself:

- Have you made note of the application deadlines, and perhaps set yourself a reminder to submit well in advance of the due date? You will want to leave enough time for your payment to go through and ensure that you receive confirmation of your submission before the deadline.

- Have you applied to at least three college or university programs, in order to have options if you don't get into your first choice?

- Do you have any idea about your likelihood of being accepted into your preferred program(s)?

- If you don't get the offer of admission that you're hoping for, do you have a Plan B? Plan C?

Parents' Note:
If your child does not get accepted into their first choice of post-secondary program, they may naturally feel quite dejected. Remind them that this does not reflect on their value

as a person, nor their likelihood of eventually achieving their goals. Ask them to consider their Plans B and C, which might take them in entirely new directions or might help them to circle back to Plan A at a later time. There are so many great educational and experiential opportunities out there for them – this is just one of many challenges that they will be able to learn from on their journey to personal success and happiness.

Living Arrangements

Being accepted into a post-secondary program does not end your decision-making process. Unless you plan to live at home, you will need to consider your preferences for living arrangements.

Applying to Residence

As described previously, living in residence has many benefits, especially for first-year students just out of high school: most university and college residences provide secure housing right on campus, with meals, social activities, sports facilities, mentors, classmates and friends all in one place. For many families, the location and simplicity of living on campus offers peace of mind and makes residence a worthwhile choice.

Residences can vary widely from one institution to another. Though most public post-secondary colleges and universities offer plenty of residence space on their main campuses, some have accommodations that are *not* on-campus, and a few small campuses have no residence at all. The residence buildings themselves may be old or new, and there may be big differences in the types of rooms offered: single, double, dorm, suite-style, apartment-style or townhouse. You may have a choice of different meal plans, which may be optional or mandatory. Different floors or different buildings may be gender-divided or co-ed, or may sometimes be dedicated to assorted social or interest-based groups. Many will be able to accommodate specific physical needs. They likely have no-smoking and mandatory vaccination policies.

Residences vary widely

This variety in accommodations will come with big differences in costs, so check their fees carefully. They will also have

Payment plans — payment plan options available.

Applications for housing in residence at most Ontario colleges and universities can be completed online as soon as you submit your program applications. You will usually find a link to apply to residence in the "campus life" section of the university or college's website. You can also indicate your interest in residence accommodations when applying to a university on the OUAC site, and the university will then send you residence information directly.

Application deadlines — Your application will require payment of a non-refundable application fee (typically $100, but not always). Application deadlines vary, but many residences recommend that you submit your application by early March. In most cases, if you are a high school student applying for the fall term, your admission to residence is guaranteed as long as you accept your room offer by June 1st. The remaining rooms will be allocated either by lottery after an application deadline, or on a first-come, first-served basis.

Fees and contracts — Your offer of a spot in residence will include information on completing your registration and submitting either a deposit/down payment (anywhere from $400 to $1000) or the first installment of your residence fees by a specific due date. You will also be required to read and sign a residence contract, which outlines the rules you must adhere to in order to stay there, much like a lease.

Many residences fill up and have waitlists for the September start to the school year. However, there are very often spots that become available as the year progresses, particularly for the start of the winter semester; if you want to move into residence after September, contact the residence itself to find out your options and deadlines for application. Some post-secondary residences accept applications for winter, spring or summer semesters on a first-come, first-served basis instead of having an application deadline.

University colleges' residences — A few universities integrate "University Colleges" that offer residences, distinctive social programs and some academic programs in a smaller community atmosphere; all students at the university are welcome as residents, whether they pursue the University College's academic program or not. Check whether these residences accept applications through the regular university residence application process, or if you must apply directly to the University College itself.

Off-Campus Housing

Many students prefer the independence of off-campus living. If you want to find accommodations off-campus, you will need to be very aware of the types of housing available in the areas close enough to commute to your classes. There are many different types of housing, as described previously in the "Institution Considerations" section of Chapter 4.

In expensive cities, the most financially feasible and abundant option is often to rent a room in a house or apartment, sharing the main living spaces with other students or a family. You may already belong to a group of friends who are interested in renting a house or apartment together and splitting the cost – this is very common in students' second and later years of postsecondary. Though it's not always possible, the best scenario for this is when each of you signs an individual lease for your separate room, so the group is not responsible for the full cost if one member chooses to leave.

When considering location, think of your personal safety and security, the availability of transportation, and proximity to grocery stores, laundry facilities and other necessities. What you can afford will be determined not only by the monthly rent, but also any additional utility costs (heat, hydro, water, internet, etc.), parking and/or public transportation fees, any furniture and household goods you will need to buy, tenants' insurance (also known as contents insurance – insurance on all the things you own, which is required by most landlords), and of course the cost of the food you will eat. Although month-to-month leases may sometimes be found, most rental accommodations require signing a one-year lease; you will still need to pay your rent even if you won't be living there for the whole twelve months, unless you are lucky enough to find someone reliable to sublet to while you're away.

Location and affordability

As mentioned earlier, look for an off-campus housing directory or listing service on your college or university's student services or campus life web page, as it will offer housing options geared specifically toward students. There are also many rental services that offer a "map view" of offerings, so you can focus on the properties closest to your school. See if you can find out when the optimal time to look for housing will be for that area – in some cities you're best to start looking early, as landlords prefer to line up their future tenants well ahead of time; in other places, there may be a flood of available housing in the month or two before school starts. If you're looking for a rental in a city with a low vacancy rate, which is now very common in Ontario, you can expect to spend a lot of time making calls or sending emails to prospective landlords. You may feel like you're facing a lot of rejection, but be persistent, and be prepared to do lots of searching before signing a lease on a place that works well for you.

Rental applications and leases

Many rental properties require all potential tenants to fill out a rental application if they are interested in leasing a unit. Since young students typically have a very low income, they sometimes find that a rental application requests the name and information for a parent or other employed adult who will act as a guarantor, ensuring that the rent will be paid. If the landlord agrees to rent to you, you will be required to sign a lease, which is a binding contract outlining the rights and responsibilities of both the landlord and the tenant. "Fixed term" rental leases usually last for one year, but can be for any length of time that both the landlord and tenant agree to. Read the lease carefully, to be sure you understand and agree to the monthly payments (including any utilities, such as heat, hydro, water, internet, parking, etc., that must be paid in addition to the rent), as well as what you will and won't be allowed to do within the rental unit.

With the acceptance of your application, most rental properties will require you to pay both your first month's rent and your last month's rent to secure the rental unit.

If you have signed a one-year lease and you want to stay after your year is up, you can either sign a new lease for another year, or your tenancy can simply continue as a month-to-month lease. You usually must give at least sixty days' notice to the landlord whenever you plan to move out, whether it's at the end of a yearly or a monthly lease. Some landlords, however, will prefer that students sign a new lease for another full year, which might give you peace of mind if you are sure you'll want to stay at least that long.

Choosing a Roommate

Roommates can make or break your enjoyment of post-secondary life, both on and off campus.

Who you might end up living with is a particularly important factor for many when they think about living in residence, especially if they may be spending eight months in a dorm room. Some are excited to make new friends; others fear a potentially less-than-friendly relationship. Of course, in pretty much every residence, you are welcome to room with someone you already know, if both of you want to stay in the same style of room and *both* of you make that roommate request.

Some residences require you to create a personal profile of information about yourself, answering questions about your age, program, preferences and habits (like studying, socializing and cleanliness), so that they can match you up with someone similar as a roommate. On the other hand, many residences offer you the opportunity to choose your own roommate(s) before you move in. If you choose to use this service, you will post the requested profile information on a safe online platform, and from there you can message others who sound like possible matches and agree to room together if you find someone you feel comfortable with. It's kind of like online dating! It's important to be honest in your own profile – don't say you're a night owl who enjoys partying during the week if it's really not true, as you'll probably end up with a roommate that you're not compatible with. Also, don't be afraid to turn down someone's roommate request if you're not sure how good you feel about them. You will have the best outcome if you spend plenty of time reading others' posts carefully, initiating lots of contacts, and asking lots of questions. If you choose not to use the roommate-matching platform, the residence will select a roommate for you instead. If you find you're having any difficulty getting along with your roommate, talk to your residence advisor about it before it gets out of hand.

Roommate matching services

Looking for a roommate for off-campus housing can be tricky, as you may have very little opportunity to get to know the other potential occupants until you move in. You may get a glimpse of your future roommates or housemates when touring the property, or you may be able to determine a bit about the cleanliness or food habits of those already inhabiting the unit by what you see around the place. It's always recommended to have someone accompany you when viewing potential properties or when interviewing potential roommates, not only for safety's sake but also simply to have a second set of eyes that might notice something that you did not. And trust your intuition: if you're unsure that someone or someplace feels quite right, go with your gut and just say "no thanks." Having any concerns about your roommates or your accommodations while at school is definitely something to avoid.

Trust your intuition!

Course Registrations

You've applied, been accepted, and paid a tuition deposit for the coming semester. At some point after that, your to-do list will probably include registering for classes. Perhaps the program you'll be following will have a pre-determined set of courses, or perhaps you will have some leeway to choose from a list of required or suggested courses. Either way, there will probably be some further online registrations to complete.

The timing for course registrations varies widely from one institution to another: some will open up a registration portal in the late spring, while others will wait until August. Some will open for all students at midnight on a certain day, while others will give students a designated registration period specific to their year and/or their program. In a few extreme instances, getting online to register as soon possible is key to not only getting the timetable you want, but even finding a single spot in high-demand course. Delays in starting and submitting course registrations might cause regret later.

Course registration timeslots

Some students, particularly those in college, will be given a pre-set course schedule, in which case they may not have to go through a course registration process at all. If the students in these programs are divided into two or more groups, called *sections*, then the different sections will take the same courses but with different timetables; sometimes these students have the option of choosing whichever section's timetable they prefer when they register. *Course sections*

Often, students are supplied with a timetable of courses, and then can make changes to it if they wish, switching to an alternate section of a course or dropping a course altogether and registering for a completely different one. When making such changes, be very mindful of the requirements for your program, and be certain that a course you want to drop is not actually a prerequisite to get into a course you'll need in a later year.

At some schools, students need to build their own timetables from scratch when registering for courses. Whether this will be a simple process or a complicated and frustrating one depends on the course selection platform used by the school. You will need to know which courses are required or recommended for the pathway through your program – this information will be found in some detail on the program's website. *Timetables*

Hint: a wise student who has course options will have already researched the required courses and all available selection alternatives, perhaps even having created a preferred timetable, in order to be prepared and ready as soon as registration opens.

The obligation to complete **electives** – mind-broadening courses from outside your core program – is common in both college and university. Sometimes students are given a very limited selection of electives from which to choose; other programs allow for a much wider-ranging variety of electives (for instance, "any science course or humanities course," although it sometimes happens that some interesting courses are not actually open to students who aren't in the science or humanities program). When choosing an elective, take the opportunity to learn something new and interesting, making certain that it meets the criteria for your own program and fits into your timetable. *Electives*

If you have any questions about course registrations, do not hesitate to get in touch with an academic advisor at the institution. Many larger schools have academic advisors specific to each program, who are able to explain the how and why of the courses you need to take, as well as any alternate options there may be. In addition, some students have been known to seek out advice from other students about professors to favour or to avoid. Hear- *Talk to an academic advisor!*

ing from previous students through a program's Discord or other chat group, or through a student union or "rate my professor" website, may provide some opinions to consider if you have a choice of course sections when registering for classes.

Paying for It

Tuition and other fees — The cost of post-secondary education is at an all-time high, and no significant relief is in sight for the near future. Nevertheless, a post-secondary education is very likely to reap great return on your investment over the course of your working life. To prepare yourself, it is essential that you do your homework and come up with a realistic estimate of the cost your education, including your tuition and any other mandatory fees (often called ancillary, auxiliary, incidental or material fees – watch for them, as they may not be included in the tuition fee and they may add up quickly), books and equipment, rent, food, transportation, entertainment expenses, etc. Fortunately, there are many ways to pay for all of this, particularly if you start preparing and saving early.

RESPs

If you're very lucky, you have a parent or guardian who was forward-thinking and able to invest even small amounts of money in a Registered Education Savings Plan (RESP), which will now provide some funds for your post-secondary tuition and living expenses. Be sure to thank them profusely!

Getting hold of your RESP money is fairly straightforward. But even if you don't have access to any RESP funds, it is worthwhile for you to understand how the program works, as it probably offers one of the highest returns of any investment program in Canada and its quite possible that you'll want to use it to save for your own kids' education someday.

An RESP is a registered investment that can only be used for post-secondary educational needs. An RESP account can be opened through most banks and investment companies, and a monthly direct deposit can easily be set up to make your investments simple, if you wish. If opened when a child is still small, even a $20/month investment will grow to a significant sum by the time the child graduates from high school. Even better, the government's Canada Education Savings Grant will chip in 20% of whatever your yearly investment was – free money, basically – up to $500/year, and $7200 in total. It's this 20% government grant that makes an RESP such a high-yield investment. If the child does not enter post-secondary education, the funds in the account can be returned to the investor (minus the government grant).

Free money!

If you do have funds available in an RESP set up through a bank or investment company, you should make an appointment to discuss a withdrawal plan. Accessing this investment will require some paperwork. Your investment institution will require proof of registration from your post-secondary institution; if a standard proof-of-registration form or letter is not easily found on your new school's online student information portal, you may have to contact its Financial Aid office to request one. Be aware that the process may take some time, so if you need to receive your RESP funds to pay your tuition on time, you should start the process early.

Proof of registration

Student Jobs

Most students need to work to pay for some or all of their post-secondary educational costs. Your education is an investment into you, and you'll need to *earn* your future success. How important is it to you?

Those typical, minimum-wage student jobs are often a drag, but the money does add up and the experiences – both good and bad – help you learn how, why and where work will fit into your future. Summer jobs will likely extend to four months once you're in college or university, giving you more time to earn. And part-time jobs during school semesters are abundant in many locations, if you have the financial need and the time management skills to coordinate working and getting your schoolwork done.

Here's something really worthwhile: most colleges and universities offer 10 to 15-hour/week *on-campus* jobs that are not only conveniently located to your classes anyway, but are also conveniently arranged around your school schedule. Check

On-campus jobs

your school's student employment centre and apply for on-campus employment right at the beginning of the semester.

Summer jobs programs

Both the provincial and federal governments hire students. The Ontario government runs several summer jobs programs for students, including public service summer employment, a business self-employment program, natural resources and forestry jobs, and training for students facing personal challenges. Check out the various offerings at https://www.ontario.ca/page/summer-jobs-students.

The federal government's support includes a youth summer job bank (https://www.jobbank.gc.ca/youth), research positions, education/work opportunities in the military, and the Federal Student Work Experience Program (FSWEP), which offers student jobs in many federal government departments in locations all across Canada. Specific programs for Indigenous students and students with disabilities are also available. Links to these hiring programs are found at https://www.canada.ca/en/services/jobs/opportunities/student.html. The federal Youth Digital Gateway is also a hub for many training and employment opportunities for youth: https://www.youth.service.canada.ca/en/programs.

Employment centres

Another option is to visit the employment centre closest to you (find it at https://www.jobbank.gc.ca/findajob/employment-centres). An employment counsellor can help students prepare for and proceed with their job search.

Scholarships and Bursaries/Grants

Scholarships and bursaries, or grants, are funds given to cover post-secondary tuition and expenses, and do not need to be repaid. If you have decent grades, or if you are Indigenous, a Crown Ward, the first generation to go to post secondary in your family, or if you have a disability, are on social assistance, or are working for a cause like the environment or your community, there is free money out there for you. Thousands of scholarships and bursaries are offered by post-secondary institutions, businesses and private organizations. And believe it or not, hundreds of thousands of dollars in scholarships and bursaries go unclaimed every year – if you manage to earn some of this free money for school, don't forget to go pick it up! And if you receive funds from a private business or organization, remember to be considerate and always show your gratitude with a short thank you letter.

What is the difference between a scholarship and a bursary? Scholarships are usually earned based on grades (being good at school) and often also on your leadership or volunteer activities. Making an effort to get involved in these kinds of experiences during your high school years may result in welcome funding for post-secondary. Bursaries (grants), on the other hand, are generally distributed according to financial need. Small scholarships or bursaries may also be provided for those who've earned a spot on a college or university sports team. If there's a chance that you may qualify for either scholarships or bursaries or both, then think of your applications for these awards as a job, spending the time and doing what it takes to get that income!

Scholarships vs. bursaries

Scholarships

Since many scholarships are interested in your volunteer, leadership and other extracurricular activities, it is helpful to have an "experiences inventory" at hand when applying. This is a list with descriptions and pertinent details (names, dates and contact information) of any volunteer and paid work, club memberships, knowledge and skill-development experiences, and sports and other team activities you've been involved in. Of course, the easiest way to create this kind of inventory is to add to it as your activities take place, which often starts with the volunteer hours you earn for high school graduation. Having this kind of information already prepared will not only help you with scholarship applications, but also with job applications through both your high school and post-secondary years.

The most convenient scholarships to win are "entrance scholarships" offered by universities and some colleges, which don't require you to fill out any applications; these are based on achieving a final grade 12 average over 80% (either in all courses or just in your core courses), and may increase in amount for even higher averages. Working hard and doing well in your high school courses can clearly pay off handsomely after graduation! In addition, some entrance scholarships are *recurring*, meaning that you will continue to be given this scholarship money every year if you maintain a post-secondary average above a certain level.

Colleges and universities provide other scholarships as well, often based on factors beyond just your grades. Your institution's Financial Aid office webpage will have information on the possibilities. If you have not yet decided on a specific post-secondary institution, it will be worthwhile to compare the scholarships that you might qualify for at all of your potential schools, as this may make a difference in which one you end up choosing.

[margin note: Financial Aid office]

There are many, many other scholarships available from businesses, service groups and professional organizations, but you must seek them out. And the earlier you start researching and taking notes on what's out there (ie, in grade 11), the better prepared you will be, especially since some scholarships have *very* early deadlines – the big Loran and TD scholarships, for example, have deadlines as early as October of the year before you start post-secondary.

Start by searching for scholarships focused on your chosen discipline. For example, if you're planning to take a community or social work program, look for scholarships focused on these areas. If you want to become an electrician or a marine biologist or an automotive designer, you might find scholarships offered by businesses or organizations that want to support their potential future employees and members.

If you have a disability or a specific talent or skill, for example, you may qualify for provincial government or private scholarships (or bursaries) that relate to your circumstances in some way. You may also find scholarships connected to the activities of your family members. Your parent or guardian may be employed by a company that offers a scholarship, or they may belong to a professional organization or union that offers scholarships to the children of their members. If your grandparent belongs to a golf club or a community theatre group, there may be scholarship money available. Some student employers, such as McDonald's, Sobeys or Tim Hortons, offer scholarships to their working students. Even businesses that your family deals with, such as an insurance company, financial management company, realtor or grocery store may offer scholarships for their clients' youth. It's worth finding out – this is one of the few times in life when asking for free money is actually expected.

Scholarships sometimes require effort on your part, even beyond the research needed to find them. An application may ask you to write a short essay on a specific topic, or perhaps write a description of why you deserve their money. This is your opportunity to impress them by talking about your future plans, and including any relevant school or community involvement in volunteer activities, sports teams, clubs, etc.

Scholarship Application Tips:
- Keep track of scholarship due dates, and plan ahead. Do not miss a deadline!
- Neatness matters – triple-check your application for errors, and ask someone to edit it for you.
- Complete your application only in the format requested and in send your application only in the manner it specifically states (i.e., snail mail or email). If a mailed paper application is required, consider the time necessary for your application to get there when planning to meet their deadline.
- Focus on quality – only include the most important things you have accomplished.
- If you need to submit references, give them lots of time to prepare their letter. It may be useful to give them a point-form list of your accomplishments to help them write about you. Follow up with your references a week or two before the application is due to remind them of the deadline, if necessary.

Note that scholarships are not only for first-year students – there are many that are only available to upper-year students and grad students. Be sure to check your scholarship sites for postings several times every year, as application deadlines can vary widely. Scholarships are also available for Canadians studying internationally, though most are for graduate students, researchers and other working professionals – worth checking out, anyway.

Most high school guidance offices maintain a list of potential local scholarship offerings. Canadian websites that post available scholarships include Scholarships Canada (https://www.scholarshipscanada.com/), Scholar Tree (https://scholartree.ca/), Student Awards (https://studentawards.com/) and Yconic (https://yconic.com/). It's also important to keep an eye on the Financial Aid site of your post-secondary institution for their scholarship offerings and deadlines. Those who are keen to earn scholarship funds but find it difficult or stressful to navigate and manage multiple application processes may find the subscription services of GrantMe.org to be worthwhile (https://grantme.ca/platform/scholarships/).

[margin note: Scholarship websites]

Bursaries

Bursaries and grants are based on financial need, not academic merit, and you can re-apply yearly if you wish. These offerings may be smaller in number, but don't usually require a great effort to apply aside from providing a description and proof of your financial circumstances. This free money comes most often from government programs (like OSAP, in "Student Loans" below) and the post-secondary institutions themselves, although there are also some private organizations that want to help students in need. Again, look for potential bursaries or grants from businesses and organizations that has interests or goals related to you, your family, and your future career direction. You will need to fill out applications for government and school-based bursaries and grants, so check your school's Financial Aid office for more details on availability and deadlines.

Scholarships and bursaries are generally non-taxable, unless you've received more than you need to cover your expenses. (See also the "Tax Credits and Benefits" section at the end of this chapter.)

Parents' Note:
If your child is applying for scholarships, they may need your input. Some scholarships require a fair amount of work, and encouragement, help with their "experiences inventory" and support in their application process may end up saving you money on their education.

Bursary applications will likely require the inclusion of parents' income to determine the student's financial need. Supplying your financial information may help your child achieve their post-secondary goals.

Government Subsidized Retraining Programs

Our governments offer subsidized retraining programs for those who have not completed secondary school or have been unemployed or underemployed for some time.

Better Jobs Ontario provides training and financial support for people who are unemployed or are working but having difficulty making ends meet. This program's funding will cover the cost of tuition, equipment and living expenses for programs of up to one year in more high-demand occupations. https://www.ontario.ca/page/second-career

Those who are in financial need and are supported by social assistance from Ontario Works may also be eligible for assistance with education and job training. https://www.ontario.ca/page/social-assistance#section-0

You can also meet with an employment counsellor to discuss your personal situation, the work or training programs available to you, and job prospects in your area. Find your closest employment centre with the search tool at https://feat.findhelp.ca/.

Student Loans

Only accept a loan if you really need it – it's better not to start your working life in debt if it can be avoided. That said, about half of post-secondary students are in debt when they graduate. In Ontario in 2015, the average amount of debt held at graduation by those with a college diploma was $16,500, while the average debt of graduates with a bachelor's degree was $30,000.[14] Applying for government student aid is generally a good idea, because you can later choose not to take the loan (but can still take a grant, if offered) and you will be giving yourself a safety net in case you run out of money.

Government Student Aid Programs

Both the federal government of Canada and the government of Ontario provide a variety of loans and grants for full-time and part-time post-secondary students, depending on your family income and your expected academic and living expenses. Unless you are considered "independent," it is anticipated that your parents will offer some help financially, if they are able; also, if you are married, your spouse's income will be considered. All income information will be verified with Revenue Canada, so ensure that the amounts entered on your application form are as accurate as possible. Grants do not require repayment, and you will not be required to start repaying your student aid until you're employed, six months after you stop attending school.

[margin note: Federal gov't loans and grants] The federal government's Canada Student Financial Assistance Program provides assistance to post-secondary students of any age, and there are additional loans and grants for those with disabilities, those with dependants, those from low-income families, and those undertaking specific apprenticeship programs. Information about the federal government's role in student aid can be found here: https://www.canada.ca/en/services/benefits/education/student-aid.html. You will automatically be assessed for a Canada Student Loan when you apply for a provincial student loan program, so there is no specific application paperwork for a Canada Student Loan from the federal government.

[margin note: Trades grants] The federal government also offers financial supports specifically for those entering the trades (https://www.canada.ca/en/services/jobs/training/support-skilled-tradesapprentices/grants.html), including incentive grants for women, and loans for Red Seal trades apprenticeships (https://www.canada.ca/en/services/jobs/training/support-skilled-trades-apprentices/loan.html).

The provincial student loan program in Ontario is known as OSAP, the Ontario Student Assistance Program (https://www.ontario.ca/page/osap-ontario-student-assistance-program). OSAP awards both loans and grants to Ontario residents, with additional funding available to those who are Indigenous, have a disability, are/were a Crown ward (in government care), or are receiving social assistance. Further information is available here: https://www.ontario.ca/page/osap-for-under-represented-learners. Sometimes special funding is also offered to students preparing for certain high-demand occupations or extending their learning through micro-credentials. Your high school may offer an OSAP presentation; if so, be sure to attend and take notes.

OSAP

You can apply for government student aid every year. You can even get an estimate of how much money you're likely to receive by using the OSAP calculator, and can then decide whether you can afford to go to school or not. Using money from an RESP will not affect how much OSAP you can get.

It's best to submit your application as soon as you've decided to pursue your post-secondary education, since the process can take some time, and you can always make changes or cancel it if you change your mind. Before starting your first application for OSAP, you will be required to complete a 15-minute information module, to be sure you understand how the program works and your own responsibilities in receiving this government assistance. Be prepared to provide fairly detailed financial information, including that of any parent, guardian or spouse supporting you, when filling out your application.

Applying

Applying for OSAP may be somewhat quicker if you link your OSAP application to your university or college application, though it's not required to do so at that time.

If you are eligible for a grant, you can request grant-only funding and turn down the loan portion of the assistance you've been offered, if you wish. Again, the Financial Aid office at your college or university can help with this.

You may also be eligible for student aid if you're planning to study outside of Ontario, or even outside of Canada. You can check whether your future post-secondary institution is approved for funding at https://osap.gov.on.ca/SchoolSearchWeb/search/school_search.xhtml?commonTask=Y. If not, you can request that it be added to the funded list with this lengthy

Student aid for interprovincial or international study

(but potentially lucrative) form: https://osap.gov.on.ca/prodconsum/groups/forms/documents/forms/tcont003568.pdf.

Student aid for out-of-province or international study involves dealing directly with the Student Financial Assistance Branch of the Ministry of Colleges and Universities, instead of using the regular online portal.

Upon receiving a government student loan, you will be registered with the National Student Loans Service Centre (NSLSC), who will maintain your loan contract and, eventually, contact you to outline your full loan amount owing, interest rate, and minimum monthly repayment schedule. You will need to start paying back what you owe six months after you graduate, withdraw from your post-secondary institution or reach your lifetime student aid maximum, although extensions of the 6-month grace period are possible if your income is low. You must communicate with the NSLSC about any changes in your status and ability to meet your repayment obligations. Find out more about repaying your loan at https://www.canada.ca/en/services/benefits/education/student-aid/grants-loans/repay.html.

National Student Loans Service Centre

Bank and Private Loans

Many banks, credit unions and other lending companies offer student loans or student lines of credit, although these tend to have higher interest rates than government student loans and interest will begin to be charged as soon as you receive the money.

If you find yourself in a pickle and don't have the funds to pay for tuition or buy the required equipment by the deadline, ask the Financial Aid office about an emergency loan. Most schools will provide a short-term loan for certain situations, such as a lag time between being accepted for a student loan and waiting for the OSAP to arrive.

Emergency loans

No matter who lends you the money, avoid "blowing" your student loan. Too many students misuse their money early in the school year, then find themselves short in March. Make a budget and stick to it. The less you have to pay back after post-secondary, the better.

Again, having a student loan through a government program or a bank provides you with the opportunity to pursue a post-secondary education, which is a great investment in your future.

Doing what you can to earn money through work and scholarships or grants will help you to graduate with minimal student debt, starting your career in the best situation possible.

Tax Credits and Benefits

As always, you are likely to pay taxes on your income while you're a student if you earn more than the federal and provincial minimums for the current tax year ($14,398 for federal taxes and $11,141 for provincial taxes in 2022), depending on your deductions and tax credits. The governments of Ontario and Canada both give tax benefits and credits for education and training fees and other expenses related to your post-secondary education. Eligible full-time and part-time students may claim educational expenses when they've attended a qualifying post-secondary educational program.

Grants and loans are income

As mentioned, most scholarships and bursaries are non-taxable (ie, they are not included as income) unless they add up to more than you actually needed to cover your expenses. Grants that you may have received for an apprenticeship program must be included as taxable income, though the cost of tools may be considered a deductible expense. RESP payments that you received are also considered income.

There are certain tax deductions that may be applied in order to *reduce your income* while a student, including moving expenses and childcare expenses. Your eligibility for these tax deductions depends on your personal circumstances, so be sure to get the details from the Canada Revenue Agency.

Tax deductions and tax credits

There are also some tax credits that pertain to post-secondary students. You will likely be able to claim the cost of tuition paid during the year as a tax credit, which means it is *applied against the taxes that you owe* because of your income. If a student's rate of tax owing falls to zero, then any extra tuition fees not used when the student files their own tax return can be saved to use on a future tax return. Alternately, up to $5000 of the student's unused tuition claim can be transferred to a parent to use on their own tax return. All post-secondary institutions must make Form T2202 available to you by February 28th – this official form shows the fees that were paid during the tax year. Most schools post this on your personal account on their

Form T2202

websites, so you can download it to use when filing your taxes.

When you are no longer a student, you may be paying back a student loan that you had received previously; if that's the case, you can claim a tax credit for the interest portion of those loan payments, in order to reduce your tax bill. If you do not have to pay taxes for the year the interest is paid, you can carry that "interest paid" amount forward for up to five years to use on future tax returns.

If you are a low-income student paying rent to live off-campus or paying on-campus residence fees, you may be able to claim the Ontario Energy and Property Tax Credit. If you paid rent in Northern Ontario, you may also qualify for the Northern Ontario Energy Credit. These are both part of the Ontario Trillium Benefit program, which would send you a refund either monthly or yearly. To apply for this credit, fill out the Ontario Trillium Benefit application form when you file your taxes (Form ON-BEN). For other tax credits that may also apply to you, check out the Canada Revenue Agency's tuition tax credit page, at https://www.canada.ca/en/revenue-agency/services/tax/technical-information/income-tax/income-tax-folios-index/series-1-individuals/folio-2-students/income-tax-folios1-f2-c2-tuition-tax-credit.html#toc44.

The Canada Revenue Agency has also created a comprehensive guide to taxes for students: https://www.canada.ca/en/revenue-agency/services/forms-publications/publications/p105/p105-students-income-tax.html

Student tax guide

When tax season comes around, low-income earners (like the majority of students) may be eligible to have their taxes done by volunteers at one of the federal government's free tax clinics (https://www.canada.ca/en/revenue-agency/ services/tax/individuals/community-volunteer-income-tax-program/need-a-hand-complete-your-tax-return.html). Some tax filing software companies also offer their products for free to post-secondary students, people under age 25, low-income earners, or those wishing to file simple tax returns online (for example, UFile-FREE, TurboTax Online, GenuTax, CloudTax). Take advantage of the information offered by the Canada Revenue Agency to reduce your tax load and put more of your money toward your education.

Parents' Note:

If your child has a paying job while in high school, this is a great opportunity for them to learn how to complete and submit their taxes while it's relatively simple. Taxes for post-secondary students are slightly more complicated, with the deductions and credits described above, and the Canada Revenue Agency's guide to taxes for students will come in handy. Remember, if your child does not need to use all of their tuition to reduce their claim and lower their taxes owing, you can use up to $5000 of the remainder to reduce your own tax bill.

Questions to ask yourself:

- Do you have a source of funds that will cover your post-secondary expenses?
- If necessary, are you willing and able to work while taking courses, earning enough money to cover your expenses?
- If needed, do you qualify for a Canada Student Loan?
- Are you willing to do the work necessary to research and apply for potentially lucrative scholarships and bursaries? Have you started an "experience inventory" to make your applications easier?
- Do you qualify for any other forms of student assistance?
- Do you understand the ways that post-secondary students can save money when filing taxes?

6

LAUNCHING
(Adulting 101)

Launching into college or university is when your practical and life skills get put to good use, and you learn many new ones that will help you do well and enjoy the years to come.

You might discover that post-secondary life is not as scary as you'd imagined, or that you've met some great new friends, or that what you're studying is really very interesting. On the other hand, you might realize that you don't actually like the program you're in, or that being with your family back home means more to you than you thought, or that your new life is a struggle and you need to ask for help, even though it may be hard to do.

You will likely make some mistakes. You will likely make a few poor choices. You will likely face some challenges and have to learn how to overcome them. The vast majority of post-secondary students have their ups and downs, question their decisions, and take some time to settle into positive, pleasant and productive routines. You are certainly not alone in this.

Your transition to your post-secondary life begins long before your first class. Almost all post-secondary institutions offer resources to prepare you for what's to come and help you ease into your "new normal." Read through any communications you receive from the school that may outline transition programs for incoming students, and watch your school's webpage for updates on any summer orientation or "smart start" programs being offered. Take advantage of these virtual or on-campus opportunities to learn more and plan for the academic and campus life activities that will be available to you once the semester begins.

[margin note: Transition programs]

If you will be attending university in Ontario, you can find out what academic and campus life resources are available at your future school on the school's website (and often also on the residence website). If you are off to college, you can check your future school's website for new student open houses or orientation events. The more you know, the better prepared and more confident you will be! The OUAC site's university resources list (https://www.ouac.on.ca/university-student-transition-resources/) includes tables that show some of the learning and student experience support you'll find if you're registered at a university; all colleges in Ontario will have similar facilities.

Most campuses and student unions will organize some orientation events during the first week(s) of the semester, and residences will do the same for their tenants. These activities might include tours and workshops, program-specific functions, sport and club information fairs, concerts and other social events. This gives new students the opportunity to learn their way around, meet people, and have fun before getting down to the nitty gritty of academics.

Once you've settled into your new digs, shelled out on textbooks and found your classes, your post-secondary journey is underway! You are now officially a post-secondary student, investing in your future. Remember your responsibilities, look after your personal wellness, and take advantage of all that your new life has to offer.

Academics

New interests, new friends, new independence – these are all happy by-products of starting your post-secondary education, but... you are in school to *learn*. You must prioritize your schoolwork in order to see a good return on the time and money you are investing in your future.

What, exactly, do you need to *do* to be successful in your courses? This list is probably no surprise:

- Read through the course outline or syllabus for each of your courses, so you'll know what you will learn ("learning out-

On-campus resources and orientation

comes"), what you will be expected to do in order to demonstrate your learning (assignments, tests, etc.), and how you will be graded.
- Create a colour-coordinated schedule, timetable or agenda that includes your class times and your test and assignment due dates, as well as your work schedule, sports/club activities, social events, etc., so you can easily see what's coming up and plan the required time you'll need to complete your work.
- Prepare for classes – plan plenty of time to complete any readings or other course content that needs to be done before each class.
- Attend classes – arrive on time with all the tools you need, remain focused, take effective notes, participate in discussions and group work, and ask questions.
- Frequently review your notes and reflect on what you've learned in order to retain it in your memory.
- Organize your course information, deadlines and due dates, course content, notes and other study tools, textbooks, etc., so everything is easy to find and refer to when doing homework and studying for tests.
- Complete all practice questions and other work that has been given, to solidify new information or processes in your memory and your understanding.
- Start to work on assignments and projects well in advance of their due dates, giving you time to ask questions, make changes, and avoid last-minute panicking.
- Start to study for tests and exams well in advance, again giving you time to ask questions, absorb information, and avoid last-minute panicking.
- Identify if you are procrastinating and get help developing strategies to overcome it.
- Plan for plenty of down time – social activities and "me time" will give your brain a rest and make your post-secondary life enjoyable.

Tips for academic success

The atmosphere and expectations in post-secondary education are very different from those in high school: at college and university, your professors' job is simply to offer you the opportunity to learn, not to force you or "baby" you along. That said, the vast majority of professors are kind and personable, willing to help students out of tough predicaments, and wanting their young protégées to do well. They will not speak to your parents. You might be lucky to have small classes and work groups where it's easy enough to get to know everyone, including the teacher. On the other hand, especially in your first year or two, you might find yourself in huge classes with hundreds of students and multiple lab sections overseen by teaching assistants. Either way, connecting with your professors, teaching assistants or other instructors will be your first step if you're having academic difficulties. It's hard to get help if no one knows you need it. Beyond that, show even greater self-efficacy by seeking out your school's student support services.

Remember, as an adult post-secondary student, *you* are almost entirely responsible for your success. Neither your professors nor your family is in control of this, and they cannot be expected to keep you on track. Managing your work, and getting it done well and on time, is a huge change and often a great challenge for post-secondary students. Arranging for support, reminders and encouragement from friends, family and/or student services is a very responsible idea.

You are responsible for your success!

Poor self-regulation is the number one weakness that affects students' success in college and university. Having effective organizational habits plus the self-discipline to do all the necessary work competently and on time will almost certainly lead to academic success, yet these things are often lacking in new students. Because this is an unfortunate but obvious reality in the post-secondary realm, a variety of academic "student success" resources are widely available to every student at each college and university in Ontario. These can be seen as a "how-to" centres for productive student behaviours. Do you need help figuring out how to keep your course information organized, how to take useful notes, how to write essays or reports, how to study effectively for tests, how to reduce anxiety, how to manage working in groups....? You can get the support you need to do well.

Academic success resources on campus

Contacting or dropping in at the academic support or student success office at your college or university will give you the best opportunity to find assistance and improve your likelihood of academic success. The services offered there generally include small-group workshops or one-on-one assistance with a range of study and learning skills, including time management and test preparation tips; stress and coping tools; writing, math and science support; organizational aids, and procrastination-busting strategies. Many offer a free or low-cost peer tutoring service, study groups, exam prep, and mentorship programs. You may also be able to get academic help or referrals from the coordinator or administrative office of your specific program.

There are other services available on campus to help students achieve success in their education. Each institution will have an accessibility office or accessibility administrator to help students with physical disabilities that may affect their learning, including mobility on campus and accessibility aids for both online and on-campus classes. Any student who experiences learning challenges can seek accommodations meant to make access to academic success equitable for all. Most post-secondary student services offices also offer counselling for both educational and personal issues, and can refer students to off-campus facilities for learning disability testing, counselling and comprehensive mental health services.

The many academic and personal wellness services offered on Ontario campuses are free or very low cost and geared specifically to post-secondary students' needs – they are meant for *you*, so make use of the available assistance to improve your academic achievement and your personal wellbeing.

Parents' Note:
Try to check up on your child's academic progress regularly. It is not uncommon for young students who are experiencing difficulties to try to hide this information from their family, out of embarrassment or shame. Make it clear that you understand the challenges your child might be facing, and keep both an open mind and open lines of communication in case things turn sour. Remember, you may have high hopes and high expectations for your child, but this is probably all new for them and they may have to make many mistakes in order to learn how to manage their path. Encourage them to persevere and to seek out the support available.

All that said, don't forget to take breaks and have some fun, too! Balance is essential: it is well-documented that students' enjoyment of life and feeling a sense of community while in post-secondary education very strongly affects their academic achievements![15]

Questions to ask yourself:
- Do you have strong study habits that will ensure your academic success?
- If necessary, are you willing to seek help to improve your academic skills?
- Do you know where to access the help you might need?
- Do you make the effort to get involved in activities at your school beyond your academics?

Food and Shelter

Students living in residence and taking advantage of a meal plan have their essential food and shelter requirements taken care of, for the most part. By the end of the year, many have grown tired of residence food and residence life in general and look forward to a more independent living situation the following year. Living in residence does provide ease and stability in having their basic needs met, however, and a significant number of students will take advantage of this by continuing with residence life in their upper years.

What will you need to take with you when you move into residence? The website for your residence should tell you what furniture is already provided, and some will even show you the dimensions of your room in case you plan to bring extra furniture or buy an extra rug or curtains before you get there. At a minimum, a residence will provide each tenant with a bed, desk, chair, a couple of drawers for clothing, and some closet space. They might also give you a desk lamp, a garbage can and a couple of shelves. Some students look forward to decorating their new space, while others can't be bothered.

What will you need to take to residence?

You will definitely need to bring your own towels, toiletries and bedding (check what size your bed will be – some residences have extra-long twin or double beds, and those sheets can be trickier to find). If you're going to have a roommate, it is recommended to coordinate with them about shared items like soap, toilet paper and a shower curtain (if not provided), as well as sharing the cost of items that can sometimes be rented through the residence, like a small fridge or a higher-speed internet plan. The residence laundry facilities may require you to purchase a specific type of detergent for use in their machines.

Many students in residence would like to prepare their own food on occasion, or at least maintain a hoard of snacks, and your cooking and food storage ability will depend on the style of your residence room. Suite-style rooms usually have a small kitchen area with a fridge, sink and microwave, and townhouses are equipped with a stove/oven. Students often bring toasters, kettles, coffee makers, inductions cooktops, toaster ovens, and small fridges or freezers, along with all the necessary kitchenware, when they move in – check to see what is allowed. Townhouse residences each have a full kitchen, though it may feel inadequate for the number of students in the unit. Dorm rooms vary widely in size, but are often too small for more than a small fridge, toaster and kettle. No matter the style of residence, all appliances brought into a residence must be CSA approved and have an automatic shutoff for fire safety – many residences will check the acceptability of your appliances as you move in. Lists of suggested items for residence are readily available on the internet, although things like a shower caddy or a power bar could easily be overlooked.

What will you need when living off-campus?

What you will need to take when moving into an off-campus apartment or shared house will depend on whether your accommodation is fully, partly or not at all furnished, and even then can vary greatly. You will need a bed; a dresser, cabinet or shelves for clothing; a desk and chair for working; a table to eat at and someplace comfortable to sit and relax. Are these furniture items already there? Are curtains or blinds included? Clarify with your landlord what appliances are in place in the kitchen and whether or not dishware, cooking tools or other kitchen utensils are included (they are usually not).

Do as much planning in advance as possible, so your move-in can go smoothly and you can spend more time enjoying your surroundings and getting started on your classes and less time scrambling to buy batteries, dish soap and Fruit Loops.

Finding Your People

You've moved in. Now what? Since one of the most important factors in your satisfaction with your post-secondary experience is likely to be your sense of belonging within a community, you need get out there and find "your people."

Living in residence, it will prove relatively easy to meet other new students. Aside from your roommate or housemates, residence social committees tend to organize an assortment of events during the first days and weeks of school to encourage you to get out of your room and get active in the residence community. You are under no obligation to join in, but getting to know some of the others in your building early on may help you feel comfortable in your new surroundings, and keeping busy might also stave off any inklings of homesickness. Residences typically also have older students living in res and working as Residence Advisors (R.A.s, or Dons), who are available to provide support and advice to students as needed.

You might find your favourite people among those with whom you're living. Whether you live on-campus or off, getting along well with your roommate(s) or housemates can prove challenging, especially as the year moves along and course stress levels increase. An open and cooperative introductory group meeting is essential to establish an understanding of everyone's comfort level right from the start. Sit down with everyone else who shares the living space to talk honestly about everyone's needs and expectations. The two most contentious issues among roommates are usually noises and messes: when will each of you need quiet to study and sleep, how do you feel about outsiders being in your shared space, and how bothered are you by mess or grime? How will you communicate with each other if you're experiencing a problem? Together, write down and share a document establishing the agreed-upon

A group meeting is essential!

"house rules" governing behaviour expectations that ensure everyone's comfort, as well as a schedule for undertaking important tasks like cleaning the kitchen and bathroom, removing garbage, etc.

The student government or school administration at your institution might also arrange welcoming activities for all students at the beginning of the semester, including campus tours, faculty or program "meet and greets," athletic or cultural events, and other fun activities. Taking part in such activities is a good way to get to know your school and meet other students like you.

Make an effort to meet others

Joining a club, trying out for a school team, or signing up for a recreational sports league is another way to develop a sense of belonging, as your affiliation with a team or club will put you in contact with others like you. Some schools have so many options for extracurricular activities that you may be overwhelmed by the choices – everything from robotics, hockey, e-sports and racing teams to film, debate, theatre, international student or faith-based clubs might be offered – and you are likely welcome to start up a new club if your interest isn't on the list. This also presents the opportunity to try something completely new to you, expanding your experiences and skills along with your involvement in the school community.

Making new friends is not easy for everyone. The great thing about post-secondary education is that you've chosen a specific program that interests you, and the other students in your classes have chosen the same thing. You are now surrounded by people who have at least one interest in common with you! If you are naturally shy you might find it intimidating to initiate a conversation, but just smiling and saying "hey, what do you think of this class" to the student sitting next to you opens a door to a potential new friendship. Making positive social connections is one of the fundamental ways to feel happy about your post-secondary experience.

In fact, a huge indicator of student success in college is involvement. "The greater the student's involvement in college, the greater will be the amount of student learning and personal development" and those who live on campus, participate in sports or clubs, or maintain part-time jobs on campus have been shown to perform best.[16] Getting involved with school clubs, sports, jobs and other social activities increases students' satisfaction with their post-secondary life, which generally leads to more positive feelings and behaviours when it comes to their academics, which leads to overall post-secondary success. A key step toward achieving more in college or university is simply getting out there and finding ways to join in.

Your Health and Safety

Launching into post-secondary life can be full of challenges and create mental health issues for many students, young and older. Anxiety, stress and depression are the top mental health issues among post-secondary students,[17] and all public colleges and universities offer mental health resources for students.

A very high proportion of post-secondary students experience stress and anxiety.[18] What exactly is stress? Stress is the way our minds react emotionally and our bodies react physically when we face some sort of challenging situation. It's a biological, hormonal reaction. Just thinking about potential stressors makes your body respond as though you are experiencing them, and if you can't stop thinking about them, the stress becomes generalized anxiety. We know that anxiety can take a toll on your health over time.

Stress resulting from academic pressures may actually impede academic performance. Too much to do and not enough time to do it tops the list of academic stressors – that's why time management is such a big topic among students, and why a growing number of students choose to take a reduced course load, even though it may take longer to graduate. Stress can lead you to emotional reactions like anger, apprehension or sadness; physiological reactions such as increased blood pressure and sweating, insomnia, headaches or exhaustion; and behavioural reactions like aggression, poor eating habits, or escapism through drugs or alcohol. Stress can also affect your academics directly: it can reduce your attention span, reduce your ability to think critically, and impede your capacity to retain new information or retrieve it from your memory.

Academic stressors

You can learn and practice coping strategies to help you now and in the future. For example, when first faced with a problem and before allowing it to fester in your mind, put it into perspective: how serious is it, really, and how much will it really affect your future? Recognize that your initial emotional reaction to a problem may be fear and apprehension, which may be unnecessary or even irrational, and you can control these emotions by thinking critically about the importance of the current problem within the bigger picture of your life. With controlled emotions, you are much more capable of using your problem-solving skills (like time management, for example) to take charge of the situation.

> *Work on your coping skills*

Understanding and nurturing your mental health and coping skills as a regular part of your daily life will better prepare you to deal with stressful situations when they arise. Taking care of your physical health will, of course, help your overall state of mind. Many students take up mindfulness habits like meditation or yoga, or find other relaxation techniques to help them improve their mood, sleep better, and face their daily hassles with a less anxious emotional response. Even making an effort to go for a daily walk or get out of your room and explore your surroundings can put you in a much better mental state to deal with any stressful academic or personal situations that come up.

> *Homesickness is incredibly common!*

Homesickness among new post-secondary students is an emotional state that is absolutely normal and may take quite some time to pass – and it *will* pass eventually if you can just weather the storm. Technology makes staying in touch with your family very easy, if that helps you cope. Some advisors recommend that you spend more time being distracted with fun social activities and less time connecting with the family if that interaction actually feeds your homesickness. How you deal with these feelings depends on your own situation, though it is likely that you will receive the best encouragement and understanding by being open and honest with your family, and by seeking out the support of the student counselling services on campus. Do understand that you are not at all alone with these emotions – they are very, very common, and many of your friends and classmates will be experiencing the same thing.

Parents' Note:
Keep communicating regularly with your child, encouraging them to be open and honest about their experiences and feelings. If you notice major changes in their emotions, moods, energy, interest in school or in social connections, or their eating and sleeping habits, they may not be coping well and may need support or interventions. Watch for warning signs that all is not well, and do what you can to support them in getting help.

In addition to mental health counselling services, most campuses with medium or large populations provide a medical health clinic for all registered students. Colleges that have a dental hygiene program may also offer free dental cleanings for anyone who is interested, as part of the clinical practice for their dental hygiene students.

At many post-secondary institutions, students are automatically enrolled in a student health insurance plan when registering. A health insurance plan pays for all or part of the fees for dental care, medical supplies and equipment, prescription drugs, or some extended health benefits like physiotherapy, massage or chiropractic care. What the plan covers will vary from one school to another, and some student health insurance plans allow you to choose between different coverages, depending on what your needs are. You can opt out of this during the first month of the semester and receive a refund of the insurance plan fee if you show evidence of having other health insurance coverage (for example, through your or your parent's work benefits). *Student health insurance plans*

Our health is affected in large part by the choices that we make. We know what's good for us and what's not good for us – accurate, reliable health information is not hard to find. It is up to you to pay attention to your health, not only for your physical and mental wellbeing, but for your *academic success* as well. You may have heard the old saying, "A healthy body leads to a healthy mind." In order for your brain to function at its best both emotionally and academically, it requires three things: nutritious food, regular exercise and a consistent sleep schedule.

Eating

Nutritious foods provide fuel for your body – including your brain. Much like a finely-tuned Lamborghini needs premium, high octane fuel to keep it running smooth and fast, your brain needs premium, highly nutritious foods to keep focusing, understanding, remembering and processing information at a high level. You may be eating plenty of food, but if it's not providing the nutrients your brain needs, you will still be running on empty. Minimize the fast foods and processed, pre-packaged foods that are often high in sugars, fats, carbs, salt and preservatives, and low in the vitamins, minerals, fibre and proteins that we need. These things are fine on occasion, but not as a steady diet for your Lambo of a brain.

The new Canada Food Guide illustrates the components of a healthy diet, and the ideal proportions of each. Ideally, we should aim for about half of our food intake to be fruits and vegetables. In fact, vegetables are much more valuable than fruits, as they offer more vitamins and minerals without the high levels of sugar found in fruit. We can survive pretty well without fruits, but not so well without vegetables. About a quarter of a healthy diet will be made up of proteins, which can come from meat, eggs, beans and legumes, some nuts, etc., and another quarter will be whole grains from pasta, bread, rice, quinoa, etc. Bear in mind that whole grains are generally not white – not white bread or white rice, for instance, which no longer contain the nutritious bran and germ of the grain – whole grains are more natural, nutritious and flavourful.

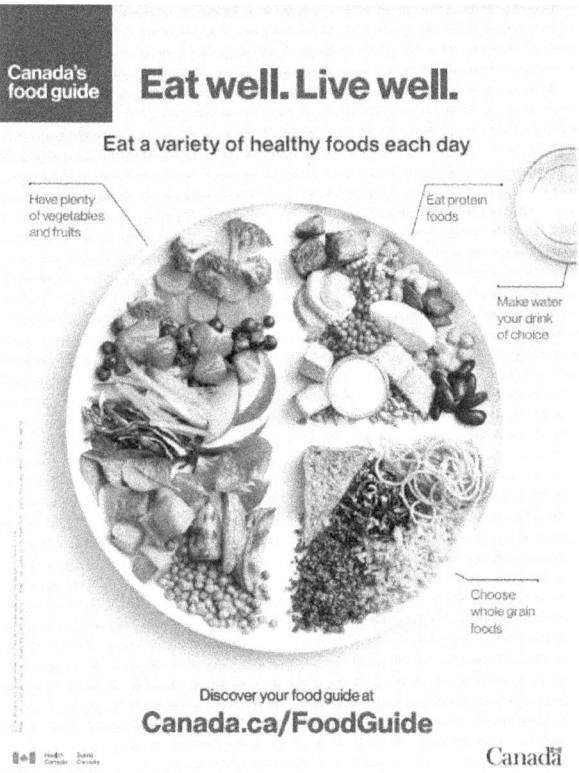

Eating healthfully is not only about what you eat, it's also about when, where, why and how much you eat. There is a psychological component to this most basic and essential function. Do you take time to sit down and enjoy a meal with others, or is eating just a necessary task among other tasks? Do you eat when you're hungry, or do you snack unnecessarily when you're stressed, or socializing, or bored? Do you eat a big meal whether you're very hungry or just a bit hungry, just because it's a routine? Do you know how much food you actually *need* to be optimally healthy? In Japan, there's a Confucian ideal called Hara Hache Bun Me, which is to eat only until you feel about 80% full. By eating slowly and deliberately, we can also give our brains enough time to register the intake and initial digestion of a meal and thus know when we've had enough before we overfill our bellies. Even fast food can be savoured and enjoyed slowly. And managing your eating habits will also help you avoid the infamous "Freshman Fifteen," the unwanted weight that many students gain during their post-secondary years.

The psychology of eating

Many students learn to cook and bake for the first time during their post-secondary years. Preparing your own simple meals with fresh ingredients can relieve the monotony of pre-packaged foods and cafeteria meals, and trying out new methods and recipes is a fun activity for many people. And then, of course, enjoy the food you've made: eat slowly and savour the flavours, knowing that you've practiced a great life skill!

Parents' Note:
Does your child know how to prepare nutritious foods? Most young adults are confident in making themselves a sandwich or heating up pre-packaged, frozen or canned foods, but may have little experience in making a meal with vegetables, meat, pasta, etc. There are plenty of cookbooks geared to inexperienced cooks – perhaps one of these would make a great Christmas or high school graduation gift for your child, giving them the opportunity to try out a few recipes and build their self-confidence before they head out on their own.

Encourage them to help with family meal preparation, and remind them that there are many ways to approach cooking and very few rules to follow (aside from safety rules, like ensuring that meat is fully cooked and that foods are refrigerated appropriately). A student who can make a decent omelette, a simple stirfry, a salad, pasta and sauce, or a pot of homemade soup is well on their way to food self-sufficiency!

Exercise

When it comes to improving your level of health, exercise is the *most significant* intervention. Exercise is also a significant factor in improving academic success, yet exercise is also often the first activity to get dropped if one's schedule starts filling up.

We all know that exercise has many health benefits, but how does regular exercise improve your academics? Aside from just strengthening your body, it strengthens you brain by facilitating brain cells' continuous reproduction and improving its memory functioning. Exercising just before studying or as a study break can also improve your focus. Intense activities such as aerobics, jogging, or brisk walking promote better circulation of the blood from your body to the brain and this, in turn, enables effective cell growth for learning and cognition. Exercise can also improve your mood, which helps when you've got homework to do.[19] You've probably experienced that feeling of not really wanting to do some exercise routine, but you know you'll feel good afterward so you force yourself to do it anyway, and then, sure enough, you do feel good afterward. Exercise increases your body's release of hormones like endorphins, which are positive and calming. Everybody likes to be in a good mood!

Exercise has a huge effect on academics!

Starting an exercise routine when you haven't been very active can be hard, and you'll need to be very careful not to overdo it and hurt yourself. Some tips to get you going include:

- writing down your fitness goal and having a plan detailing why and how you're going to achieve it
- scheduling the time you'll need for fitness
- varying your routine to include flexibility, cardiovascular and strength training to make it more interesting and well-rounded
- listening to a great playlist while you exercise
- making a fitness plan with a friend, to keep each other accountable to continuing with it

Tips on starting a fitness routine

Find a form of exercise that fits your personality, so you'll enjoy it. For example, if you're very social, try a fitness class or join one of your school's recreational teams. If you prefer solo exercise, try hiking, running, swimming, going to the gym, or online workout programs you can do at home. Consider cheap and easy forms of fitness, like dancing or walking, and choose things like biking to campus instead of driving, or taking the stairs instead of an elevator. Planning to exercise with a buddy might keep you both motivated and accountable for continuing. No matter what you do for exercise, know that every step, stretch or other movement you make will be benefitting your body, your mind, and even your grades.

Parents' Note:
Do you set a good example for your child when it comes to fitness? If you want to encourage them to be active later, show them how good it feels to be fit now. Getting some exercise together can be a great way to establish exercise routines and encourage life-long fitness. Even getting out for occasional walks together – though it may take some cajoling at first – can make you both feel good and also open up the opportunity for conversation. The hormones released through exercise relieve stress and promote social connections, so an open chat about all the upcoming life changes might be more likely after some road hockey, a bike ride, or a game of badminton in the back yard.

Sleep

How much sleep do you need? How much sleep do you get?

Adults averaged about 9 hours of sleep each night until the perfection and mass marketing of artificial light with the incandescent lightbulb. We average much less than that today, despite not having changed physically over the past century.[20] Most researchers agree that the average young adult needs at least 8 hours of sleep each night to function at their best. Many need more than that, and some can get away with less. If you rarely feel sleepy during the day, or if you tend to wake up shortly before your alarm goes off, you're probably getting the right amount of sleep each night for *you*.

Not getting enough sleep, on the other hand, is a huge problem for college students. Sometimes students' lack of sleep is simply due to procrastinating on important and urgent work on assignments or studying for tests, or the stress created by that procrastination. Many students seem to think that sleeping twelve hours a night on weekends will make up for sleeping six hours a night on weeknights. You may think you'll be fine with an erratic sleep pattern and five hours a night with an all-nighter or two thrown in now and again. You know you're kidding yourself, right?

It is known that staying up late to party on weekends instead of maintaining a consistent sleep schedule results in a significantly poorer memory of previously-studied material. In fact, according to UBC psychologist Dr. Stanley Coren, "one hour's lost sleep out of eight results in a drop of one point of I.Q. and for every additional hour lost, you drop two points. And it accumulates. So if you cheat on sleep by two hours a night over a five-day week, you've lost 15 points."[21] You may question the measuring of intelligence by I.Q., but you get the drift: lack of sleep takes away our brain power and makes us dumber. Think about that when you've got an exam to write.

Clearly, sleep deprivation can have a serious effect on your academics and your overall ability to cope with life, disrupting your moods and your ability to cope with the stressors in your life. It affects your overall physical health and even your safety by causing inattentiveness and lack of focus, which slows reaction times (much like what happens with alcohol intake) and reduces your response to environmental signals. Lack of sleep also weakens your brain's ability to function. Without enough sleep, students' ability to pay attention and concentrate are greatly reduced, as is their ability to both create and access memories. That makes it kind of hard to study! A reduction in memory, creativity and decision-making skills often leads to a reduction in grades. A chronic lack of sleep can also contribute to serious health issues like obesity, diabetes, and heart disease.[22] You don't want any of that. Establish healthy sleep routines.

Sleep deprivation has disastrous effects!

If you need to improve your sleep, there are several things you can do that are known to be helpful:

- First and foremost, be consistent. Any sleep expert will tell you that the number one way to improve your sleep is to stick to a sleep routine. That doesn't mean one bedtime for weeknights and one for weekends, it means one bedtime and wake up time for *every day.* Try not to vary it too much, so your biological clock and your body will function more smoothly.
- Exercise regularly. It's well known that exercise improves both your ability to fall asleep and the quality of your sleep.
- Turn off your electronics a minimum of half an hour before going to bed. Using blue light filters is a great idea, but,

How to improve your sleep

even so, the stimulation of screens and the information being relayed by them keeps your brain buzzing at a level that makes it harder to settle down into sleep.
- Create a ritual. Your mind and your body react better to bedtime when there is a winding-down ritual for it. For example, after shutting down your electronics, maybe have a little snack, or a warm bath, brush your teeth, get comfortable with something to read for ten or twenty minutes to wind down. You'll probably have a textbook that'll make you drowsy pretty quick! It doesn't take long for most people's bodies to get used to a winding-down routine, making it easier to fall asleep.
- Manage your sleep environment. You spend about a third of your life sleeping. Having a bed and bedding that are comfortable for you may be a big but very worthwhile investment, particularly when you think about the consequences of not sleeping well – a foam mattress topper might make a residence bed much more comfortable, for instance. Most people also sleep better in a very dark room, and in cooler temperatures. Have a glass of water next to the bed if you tend to wake up thirsty. Keep your bedding clean. And park those beeping, light-emitting electronics far away, out of your bedroom, if possible.
- Avoid coffee and caffeinated drinks after mid-afternoon, because it takes 8-10 hours to get it out of your system. Have no alcohol within a couple of hours of bedtime, because it dehydrates you and interferes with the quality of your sleep.
- If necessary, take short power naps. Many cultures encourage a nap partway through the day, when your energy level is lagging, to refresh and energize you enough to focus and enjoy the rest of your day. Note, however, that a nap is not 2 hours under the blankets in your bed. That's a full-on sleep: it'll be hard to wake up from, and it'll mess with your sleep schedule. A nap is short – 15-30 minutes, just to rest and recharge – and it doesn't take you right down into that deep sleep that'll make you groggy for the rest of the day.

Eating well, getting exercise and getting enough sleep are all clearly important for achieving your greatest success as a student. They are examples of those mature, self-regulation habits that lead you to achieving success in *all* your lifelong goals, so you will certainly want to nurture them. Starting your post-secondary education is a time of lots of changes, so why not make it a time to start some healthy new habits... or drop some unhealthy old ones: try out a new sport, bake your first cake, quit smoking, or make an appointment with a counsellor. Take the opportunity to prove to yourself (and everyone else) that you are an adult who is able to make good decisions and live well on the way to achieving your goals for the future.

Safety

Students' personal safety is of top concern at all Ontario campuses, but no one can completely control what other people do. Many post-secondary institutions have precautionary tools such as surveillance cameras, emergency phones or alarms, or campus walk programs to get you where you need to go safely. Add the campus security phone number or app to your phone. As always, you must think and act in ways that protect your safety in any situations involving other people that you don't know very well.

Gender-based and sexual violence does happen at post-secondary institutions, and is most likely to occur during the party atmosphere of orientation events during the first weeks of classes, before homework and studying become the dominant student activities. Some institutions now require all students to complete a preventive training program in consent and personal safety. Look for self-defence classes offered by your school or community, to improve your own recognition of problematic safety circumstances as well as your ability to defend yourself should you ever feel unsafe.

Don't be over-confident and overestimate your safety in new situations. Always be aware of your surroundings. Plan in advance for social activities potentially involving alcohol or other drugs, knowing that your alertness and responsiveness will deteriorate quickly whenever you are not completely sober. The best ways to stay safe are to be prepared and to reduce your likelihood of encountering an unsafe situation in the first place. That said, do not ever be afraid to seek help and support if you find yourself in a situation where you feel uncomfortable, or if you have experienced violence or any security issue, or if you have witnessed someone else in danger.

Settling Into the New Normal

Some students get into the groove of their new existence right away; others take many months to feel comfortable with their academics, social life, and day-to-day living. When you develop a routine that includes classes, dedicated study time, work (if you have a job), mealtimes and leisure, you will be astonished by how quickly time passes. Managing these different aspects of your life, with help if needed, will get you settled into effective habits that will launch you toward your goals.

Develop a routine

When a new baby is born, the first six weeks of its life are considered a transitional period for its whole family. The same can be said for the first six weeks or more after that child, now an adult, leaves the family home to live on their own. If you've left home to enter college or university, you (and the family left behind) may experience feelings of uncertainty, emptiness or bewilderment with these new circumstances. This is completely natural. You might later experience a period of awkwardness if you move back home next summer – after having lived on your own, the structure and expectations of life back with your family might actually feel annoying.

In the meantime, keep yourself busy and know that this transition may not be easy, but any feelings or awkwardness or uncertainty will pass eventually. Make the most of all the resources at your disposal to help you with your schoolwork and your mental health, get involved, and enjoy your new circumstances. If you've moved away from home, use your student bus pass to get out of your room and explore the city. If your finances are pretty tight, look for a part-time job to make a little extra spending money. If you want to meet more people like you, join a club or sign up for a recreational sports league. You are responsible for what happens now, and the opportunities available are vast. Take charge of your new normal and make it what you want it to be.

7

CHANGING DIRECTION
(If you change your mind)

What if it's not working out? What if you can't stand your program, or you hate where you're living, or you've run out of money, or you've failed your courses? What if looks like your decisions sucked?

During the first year of their post-secondary program, many, many young post-secondary students are unsure whether they made the right choices, and many of them seek counselling and advice from their student services office to deal with their stress. Most colleges and universities have these advisors available for both academic and personal issues, and can refer students to professional counselling when appropriate. If you seek help from a professional counsellor outside the school on your own, look for one that is experienced in dealing with young adults; some counsellors even specialize in helping post-secondary students get through these hurdles – that shows how common post-secondary stress is.

About ten to fifteen percent of college and university students withdraw or change programs within the first two years of their studies.[23] There are four very common reasons for students' non-completion of post-secondary education within the standard expected time frame, though, of course, there may be others depending on students' circumstances.

1. They don't like the program.

What sounded good last year might have turned out to be completely different than expected – they had no way of really knowing until they actually experienced the program. Perhaps it turned out that it wasn't really a good match with their interests, aptitudes, strengths or values. Perhaps they've been exposed to something else that piqued their interest more.

Whatever the case, the vast majority of these students who reject their initial program will eventually complete their post-secondary education in a different program, often at a different institution. Some transfer into something else directly after first or second year, while others take time off to work or travel as they reassess their goals before reapplying for school.

If you're questioning the worth of the program you're taking, you might want to go back and look through the research and notes you took before making your program decision – perhaps you will be reminded of the value of it or of something similar, or perhaps another program that was on the table at one time will now strike a chord. Or maybe you've realized that you really have no idea what it is you want to do. There's nothing like experience to make hindsight crystal clear.

A good academic advisor can help you figure out what went wrong, what a better plan might be, and whether the courses that you've completed can still be of benefit to you when you chart a new path. When you want to change gears mid-stream, it is sometimes useful to hang in there a bit longer and complete at least a part of what you started, giving you some credits you might be able to transfer and use toward advanced standing in another program (even at another school) in the future. In other cases, cutting your losses might be a more appropriate choice. If you've made your decision early in the semester, you might be able to get a refund for some of your tuition fees... however dropping out very early on might also mean that you're not giving the program much of a chance.

There are currently over 1,900 credit transfer pathways available between Ontario post-secondary institutions. The many pathways for transferring credits from one school to another can be explored here: https://search.ontransfer.ca/.

Credit transfer pathways

It might be sufficient for you to simply drop a course or two, so you can focus on doing well in the rest of your courses. If you're doing poorly in one course and you're thinking about withdrawing from it, make sure you do that before the deadline. Withdrawal deadline dates are often just before the final exam period, giving you lots of time to try to pick up the pieces and pass instead. If you're bombing out in a course, though, it may

Withdrawing from a course

be better to withdraw from it than to have an F on your transcript, which will bring down your GPA (Grade Point Average – the overall average from all your courses). Having a poor grade on your transcript could disqualify you from co-op program in later years, and a lower GPA could reduce or discontinue a recurring entrance scholarship. Check with your school's academic advising department before withdrawing from a course, to ensure that you won't face any academic penalties.

2. Poor academic performance

Students who are unprepared or ill-equipped with the self-regulatory behaviours needed for success are unlikely to do well in their courses. Some are simply not ready to take on the responsibility of post-secondary education, and unable to complete the required work and studying in a timely and effective manner. Others have a fixed mindset, and when things don't go as well as expected, they quickly give up instead of putting more effort into learning. Even if they do have strong academic skills, those who are not enjoying their classes are likely to be less engaged and less successful, giving up on their work from uncertainty or despair.

As described in the "Academics" section of Chapter 6, the student services office is where students can get advice on academic skills and study habits to improve their learning. Many schools offer study skills programs or workshops on time management, note-taking, studying, managing test anxiety, etc., and some even schedule credit courses covering student success topics. They also often arrange for peer tutors to help other students with particular courses – sign up for tutoring at the first sign of difficulty, before it gets too late to rectify the situation. It is worthwhile to find out what resources are available to help improve one's academic performance before giving up altogether.

Academic and emotional stresses can feed on each other, contributing to a student's eventual choice to drop out of their program. Often, taking time to find different, positive life experiences – whether at school or elsewhere – will eventually lead these students to greater self-awareness, self-confidence and readiness for post-secondary education... and whatever else life throws their way.

[margin note: Student Services office]

As Albert Einstein said, "Failure is success in progress." He knew this from experience.

3. Affordability

The cost of post-secondary education has grown exponentially over the past forty years – much more quickly than our incomes have grown over the same period – so it's not surprising that many students experience great financial hardship while at school.

In 2018, "20 percent of Canadian graduates with a bachelor degree finish(ed) their postsecondary career CAD $25,000 or more in debt."[24]

When facing financial stress, some students choose to drop out and work instead, or to switch to a more affordable program at a different institution. It has also become common for students to plan for an extended span of post-secondary, taking a reduced course load and working part-time to pay for their education as they go. The information on student loans and grants in the "Paying for It" section of Chapter 5 might be worth a second look.

Reduced course load

4. Lack of Social Engagement

We are all social beings to some degree, and shouldn't underestimate the importance of positive social interactions in a post-secondary program. Students who have difficulty establishing social bonds while in school are more likely to be unhappy with their lives in general and more likely to drop out. For most students, it is essential to find ways to engage with their peers in positive ways and build relationships that support them academically and socially.

Canadian students who do not feel any strong social bonds in their post-secondary milieu are more likely to drop out.[25] A student who chose to take a specific program that met their interests, aptitudes and values might still become unhappy with it if they're not making many social connections or not developing a sense of belonging within the program. Completing this program at this particular school and feeling lonely for several more years would not be a wise decision for most people, though there may be those who prefer to tough it out.

Build a sense of community

Searching for ways to build a sense of community while remaining in the program could include joining a school club or sports activity (or starting a new one), or finding more social interaction off-campus. A student services advisor might be able to offer suggestions. Alternately, switching into a slightly different program, or transferring into the same type of program at a different school, might provide a more conducive social atmosphere. Smaller schools with smaller classes tend to rate higher for student satisfaction when it comes to overall social community.

What Next?

When having doubts about continuing in your program, evaluate where you're at clearly and logically. Think again about your interests, aptitudes, strengths and values, and clarify whether your program is meeting the criteria you originally set or is very different than your expectations. You may have learned a lot more about yourself since you did your original self-reflection – perhaps the program is not different than expected, but *you* are.

What is the root of your unhappiness?

What is it that you want, and what needs are not being met by the situation you're in now? Could those needs be met by continuing on and simply making some small changes to your program, your schedule, or your social environment? Think deeply about your feelings, as they are of utmost importance. What *exactly* is causing your unhappy emotions? Have you A) allowed yourself enough time to get used to your new normal, and B) put in enough effort to find some enjoyment in your post-secondary life?

If you come to the conclusion that you've made a big mistake? Well, congratulations! You've succeeded in making a very important discovery: you've determined what will *not* work for you.

And you are certainly not alone! More than 10% of students will drop out of their post-secondary program by the end of their first year.[26] And those 10% will, instead, find a job, enroll in a different program, travel, volunteer… They will find different experiences taking them in a new direction.

Maybe you're ready for round two. You've learned a lot about yourself, found out what you don't like, and have some idea what your new direction might be. If you plan to continue on with your education, you might need to do some more program and institution research, and perhaps enquire about transferring your credits for possible advanced standing in a new program (https://search.ontransfer.ca/). Talk with an academic advisor about your new goals and how to achieve them. If, instead, you want to get a full-time job, or to take a gap year before returning to school, those options are just as great as they were before.

New direction

Or maybe it's back to square one. Do you need to go back and figure out who you are, what you want to be when you grow up, and where your future lies now? You are a different person now, and have learned from your post-secondary experiences, so taking the time to re-evaluate is also a valid choice.

Re-evaluate!

Because, remember, you have not been forced to nail down a lifelong career, you've only had to decipher your initial direction. Even if that initial direction turned out to be unsatisfactory, during this time you've still managed to gain a lot of insight about yourself and the world around you, and you've also acquired many transferable skills. This has definitely been a valuable experience. And now, with greater understanding, you can move on to deciphering your *next* direction.

Parents' Note:
Your child's feelings may be hard to understand. You may or may not remember how it felt to be 18 or 20 or 25; even if you do, the school environment, social environment and general daily life are probably very, very different for your child than they were for you at that age.

"Failure" in the first year of college or university is very common. Failure can mean not passing courses, doing poorly in courses, feeling homesick or socially uncomfortable, or just unhappy with the program or the new situation. It's not the end of the world, it's a learning experience. An expensive learning experience, but possibly a less expensive one when it happens early on than it would be to change direction later.

In fact, it may be a small blip in the overall picture of their life. It may change the road that they're on in big or small ways: they may change programs or even schools, choose to get a job and take more time to think about their direction, or simply reapply themselves in the same program with a new understanding of how to achieve the same goal they started out with. You might want to cut them some slack – it's not easy to navigate the post-secondary world.

Changing direction is never a failure, it's just choosing a different path. It's "learning from experience." So you may be going back to the drawing board now, but you're starting from a new position, seeing the options from a new angle, and launching forward with a better idea of yourself. And it *is* all about *you*. Take the time you need to plot your course, and expect many detours. Life is all about the journey!

8

YOUR TO DO LIST

Grade 9
- ❏ Start doing your required volunteer hours. Ask your guidance counsellor about opportunities that relate to your potential career interests.
- ❏ Take Your Kid to Work Day – look for an opportunity related to a potential career interest (i.e., it doesn't have to be at your parent's workplace). Ask for help from a guidance counsellor.
- ❏ Join a team, club, student council, or another extracurricular activity. Try something new! The experience you gain from involvement in new social groups, events and leisure pursuits will benefit your overall growth and maturity, and, eventually, your readiness for post-secondary.

Grade 10
- ❏ Continue volunteering in your community to gain experience and broaden your horizons.
- ❏ Continue generating new social experiences through teams, clubs and other leisure activities.
- ❏ Start saving for post-secondary and get some work experience with a part-time job, if possible.
- ❏ Talk to your guidance counsellor about doing a co-op, or about a dual credit or OYAP program.
- ❏ In addition to the courses required for graduation, take high school courses that sound interesting to you and are at an appropriate level for your abilities.

Grade 11

- ❏ Continue volunteering in your community. Ask your guidance counsellor for suggestions and try something new. Continue to take part in school and community extracurricular activities as well.
- ❏ Look for a part-time job, if you aren't already working. Even just a few hours a week will give you great experience and add to your résumé.
- ❏ Identify potential career directions, considering your interests, aptitudes, strengths, weaknesses and values.
- ❏ This is a great time to try a co-op in a position related to any potential career interests. It is also an excellent time to take a dual credit course or try out the OYAP program.
- ❏ If you have some ideas about post-secondary programs that might interest you, be careful to ensure that your high school course selections will meet the requirements for acceptance into these potential programs. If they might not, talk to your guidance counsellor about alternate methods for earning those pre-requisites.
- ❏ Start researching scholarships, bursaries and awards, maintaining a spreadsheet of their requirements and deadlines. Some scholarship applications have very early deadlines, so start requesting letters of reference from teachers, coaches, employers, mentors, etc., in preparation for them.
- ❏ Research post-secondary programs and institutions, as well as housing options, maintaining a spreadsheet of the information you gather.
- ❏ In the spring and summer, go on tours of some post-secondary institutions that interest you.

Grade 12

- ❏ Ensure that you have registered for all the courses you need for high school graduation, as well as any pre-requisite courses for post-secondary programs that interest you.
- ❏ If you can fit it into your schedule, consider doing a co-op related to your potential career path. This is also a good time to take a dual credit course or start an OYAP program.
- ❏ Continue gathering experience through volunteer work, team or club activities, and paid employment. All will be valuable on your résumé and scholarship applications, and the money you earn from your part-time work will be instrumental in helping pay for your post-secondary education and living expenses.
- ❏ Start applying for scholarships early in the year.
- ❏ Attend university and/or college open houses, if possible, and ask questions about your potential programs, housing, extra-curriculars, etc.
- ❏ Narrow down your preferences for post-secondary.
- ❏ Apply to colleges and universities at least a week before their deadlines (to ensure payment), allowing yourself lots of options.
- ❏ Apply to residences, if you're considering living there.
- ❏ Apply for OSAP.
- ❏ Carefully read all communications from the institutions to which you applied. Follow instructions about submitting any follow-up information, portfolios, etc., and about accepting offers you may receive from them.
- ❏ Make a decision about accepting your preferred offer. Complete the acceptance process and submit any deposits or other fees at least a week before the deadline (to ensure payment).
- ❏ Confirm acceptance of a residence offer, if applicable, and pay the required deposit. Take part in the online "roommate matching" service, if available. Start looking for off-campus housing, if needed.
- ❏ Continue following instructions from your college/university. Register for courses and pay fees as required.
- ❏ Acquire any new items you will need for your program and your accommodations.
- ❏ Find out about orientation activities, extra-curricular options, etc., and plan to join in. Take a deep breath, get settled, get down to work, and have fun!

RESOURCES
(All the links)

1. WHO ARE YOU

What Are You Aiming For?
- The government of Canada's Job Bank: https://www.jobbank.gc.ca/career-planning
- Labour market information and job profiles: https://www.ontario.ca/page/labour-market.
- Labour Market search tool: https://www.app.tcu.gov.on.ca/eng/labourmarket/employmentprofiles/index.asp.

2. WHEN YOU DON'T FEEL READY

The Victory Lap
- OYAP, the Ontario Youth Apprenticeship Program: https://oyap.com/
- Dual credit programs: https://www.ontario.ca/page/dual-credit-programs

The Work World
- Canadian Gap Year Association (CanGap) - https://www.cangap.ca/
- Ontario government youth employment programs: https://www.ontario.ca/page/get-help-finding-youth-or-student-job.
- Ontario government job preparation and job search resources: https://www.ontario.ca/page/jobs-and-employment).
- Employment centre search tool: https://feat.findhelp.ca/

Post-Secondary Preparatory Programs
- The Ontario government's employment upgrading options: https://www.ontario.ca/page/adult-learning.
- Virtual High School: https://www.virtualhighschool.com/index.asp
- Academic Career Entrance (ACE) courses online: https://www.acedistancedelivery.ca/
- Academic Career Entrance (ACE) general website: https://www.ontario.ca/page/adult-learning-academic-career-entrance
- The Ontario Colleges upgrading programs: (https://www.ontariocolleges.ca/en/news/resources-for-college-preparation

Travel
- Canadian Gap Year Association (CanGap): https://www.cangap.ca/

3. WHERE DOES YOUR FUTURE LIE?

- Ontario Colleges: www.OntarioColleges.ca.
- Interactive map of college locations: https://www.ontariocolleges.ca/en/colleges/college-map

Universities
- Ontario Universities: https://www.OntarioUniversitiesInfo.ca/

Military Careers and the Royal Military College of Canada
- The Canadian Armed Forces (CAF): https://forces.ca/en/
- Paid education opportunities through the Canadian Armed Forces: https://forces.ca/en/paid-education/
- The Royal Military College of Canada (RMC): www.rmc-cmr.ca
- Applying to RMC: https://www.rmc-cmr.ca/en/registrars-office/apply-now

Private Colleges
- Search tool for registered and provincially-approved private career colleges: https://www.ontario.ca/page/private-career-colleges
- Graduation, employment and satisfaction rates at private colleges: http://www.tcu.gov.on.ca/pepg/audiences/pcc/#kpi
- Links to Indigenous Institutes: https://iicontario.ca/indigenous-institutes/ and https://www.ontario.ca/page/indigenous-institutes
- Links to faith-based colleges: https://www.ontario.ca/page/private-postsecondary-schools

Apprenticeships
- Skilled Trades Ontario: https://www.ontario.ca/page/explore-trades-ontario#section-2
- Red Seal trades: http://www.red-seal.ca/trades/tr.1d.2s_1.3st-eng.html
- Ontario college programs in skilled trades: https://www.ontariocolleges.ca/en/apply/skilled-trades
- Free pre-apprenticeship training through the Ontario government: https://www.ontario.ca/page/prepare-apprenticeship
- Ontario Youth Apprenticeship Program (OYAP): https://oyap.com/
- Employment Ontario information on matching prospective apprentices with interested employers: https://www.ontario.ca/page/jobs-and-employment

Inter-Provincial and International Options
- Canadian Information Centre for International Credentials search tool: https://www.cicic.ca/868/search_the_directory_of_educational_institutions_in_canada.canada
- Links to Canadian universities: www.UniversityStudy.ca
- Colleges and Institutes Canada: https://www.collegesinstitutes.ca/our-members/member-directory/
- Ontario post-secondary institutions approved for student loans (or request for approval of an institution):

https://www.ontario.ca/page/study-abroad
- Canadian Information Centre for International Credentials: https://www.cicic.ca/973/learn_about_the_benefits_of_international_studies.canada

Distance Education – Online Learning
- OntarioLearn: www.OntarioLearn.com
- Private career college search tool: https://www.pcc.tcu.gov.on.ca/PARISSearchWeb/search.xhtml.
- eCampus Ontario: https://learnonline.ecampusontario.ca/
- Links to interprovincial distance education options: www.UniversityStudy.ca and https://www.collegesinstitutes.ca/our-members/member-directory/

Narrowing Down Your Preferences
- Ontario colleges: https://www.ontariocolleges.ca/en
- Ontario universities: https://www.ontariouniversitiesinfo.ca/
- Ontario Universities Fair: https://www.ontariouniversitiesfair.ca/
- Tours and special program events at Ontario universities: https://www.ontariouniversitiesinfo.ca/universities/events.
- Ontario College Fair: https://ontariocollegefair.ca/
- Links to Ontario college open houses, tours, etc.: https://www.ontariocolleges.ca/en/colleges/college-recruitment

Personal Considerations
- Ontario universities information for Indigenous students: (https://www.ontariouniversitiesindigenous.ca/
- Indigenous student centres and resources from the Ontario Native Education Counselling Association: http://oneca.com/transitions/colleges-and-universities.html
- Transition resource guide for students with disabilities: (https://www.transitionresourceguide.ca/blog/high-school-post-secondary).
- Accessibility resources available at each Ontario univer-

sity: https://www.ontariouniversitiesinfo.ca/accessibility
- Accessibility resources available at each Ontario public college: https://osca.ca/ontario-college-accessibility-and-disability-services/

Program Considerations
- Collaborative and associative programs at Ontario universities and colleges: https://www.ouac.on.ca/guide/collaborative-university-college-programs/

Institution Considerations
- "Key performance indicators" for Ontario colleges: https://www.ontario.ca/page/college-graduation-satisfaction-and-job-rates
- University graduation and job rates: https://www.ontario.ca/page/university-programs-graduation-and-job-rates

4. HOW TO GET WHERE YOU'RE GOING

Applications

University Applications
- Ontario Universities Information: https://www.ontariouniversitiesinfo.ca/
- Ontario Universities Application Centre (OUAC): https://www.ouac.on.ca/
- Equal consideration date for university applications: https://www.ouac.on.ca/deadlines/
- University programs that have winter or spring start dates: https://www.ouac.on.ca/guide/101-winter-admission/#winter
- University application portal for applicants who are not in high school: https://www.ouac.on.ca/ouac-105/
- Deadlines for Law, Education and Rehabilitation Sciences program applications: https://www.ouac.on.ca/deadlines/•
- OUAC Admission Information Service: https://www.ouac.on.ca/apply/referral/en_CA/referral/index

College Applications
- Ontario Colleges information: www.OntarioColleges.ca
- Ontario Colleges Application Service (OCAS): https://www.ontariocolleges.ca/en
- Search tool for college programs currently open for applications:
- https://www.ontariocolleges.ca/en/programs
- Transcript requests from some private colleges: https://careercollegesontario.ca/transcripts/

Royal Military College Applications
- RMC admissions information: https://www.rmc-cmr.ca/en/registrars-office/rmc-admissions
- RMC application site: https://forces.ca/en/apply-now/

Paying For It
Student Jobs
- Ontario government summer jobs programs for students: https://www.ontario.ca/page/summer-jobs-students
- Federal government youth summer job bank: https://www.jobbank.gc.ca/youth
- Federal government hiring programs for Indigenous students and students with disabilities: https://www.canada.ca/en/services/jobs/opportunities/student.html
- Youth Digital Gateway for training and employment opportunities for youth: https://www.youth.service.canada.ca/en/programs
- Canada Employment Centre search tool: https://www.jobbank.gc.ca/findajob/employment-centres

Scholarships and Bursaries/Grants
- Scholarships Canada: https://www.scholarshipscanada.com/
- Scholar Tree (https://scholartree.ca/)
- Student Awards: (https://studentawards.com/
- Yconic (https://yconic.com/)
- GrantMe: https://grantme.ca/platform/scholarships/

Government Subsidized Retraining Programs
- Better Jobs Ontario: https://www.ontario.ca/page/second-career
- Ontario Works education and job training assistance: https://www.ontario.ca/page/social-assistance#section-0
- Employment Ontario search tool: https://feat.findhelp.ca/.

Student Loans
- Canada Student Loans: https://www.canada.ca/en/services/benefits/education/student-aid.html
- Federal government financial support for those entering the trades: (https://www.canada.ca/en/services/jobs/training/support--skilled-trades-apprentices/grants.html
- Federal government incentive grants for women and loans for Red Seal trades apprenticeships: https://www.canada.ca/en/services/jobs/training/support-skilled-trades-apprentices/loan.html
- Ontario Student Assistance Program (OSAP): https://www.ontario.ca/page/osap-ontario-student-assistance-program
- OSAP funding for those who are Indigenous, have a disability, are receiving social assistance, or are/were a Crown ward: https://www.ontario.ca/page/osap-for-under-represented-learners
- Search tool for interprovincial and international post-secondary institutions approved for OSAP: https://osap.gov.on.ca/SchoolSearchWeb/search/school_search.xhtml?commonTask=Y
- Request that an interprovincial or international institution be approved for OSAP: https://osap.gov.on.ca/prodconsum/groups/forms/documents/forms/tcont003568.pdf.
- Repaying your loan to the National Student Loans Service Centre (NSLSC): https://www.canada.ca/en/services/benefits/education/student-aid/grants-loans/repay.html

Tax Credits and Benefits
- Canada Revenue Agency tuition tax credits:

https://www.canada.ca/en/revenue-agency/services/tax/technical-information/income-tax/income-tax-folios-index/series-1-individuals/folio-2-students/income-tax-folio-s1-f2-c2-tuition-tax-credit.html#toc44.
- Canada Revenue Agency's guide to taxes for students:
- https://www.canada.ca/en/revenue-agency/services/forms-publications/publications/p105/p105-students-income-tax.html
- The federal government's free tax clinics for students and other low-income earners: https://www.canada.ca/en/revenue-agency/services/tax/individuals/community-volunteer-income-tax-program/need-a-hand-complete-your-tax-return.html

5. LAUNCHING
- OUAC university resources for academic and campus life: https://www.ouac.on.ca/university-student-transition-resources/

6. CHANGING DIRECTION
- Ontario credit transfers and potential advanced standing: https://search.ontransfer.ca/

NOTES

[1] Statista. (2022). *Number of students enrolled in postsecondary institutions in Canada in 2019/20, by province.* https://www.statista.com/statistics/447802/enrollment-of-postsecondary-students-in-canada-by-province/

[2] Dr. Seuss. (1990, January). *Oh, the places you'll go!* Random House Children's Books.

[3] Statistics Canada. (2015, November 27). *An Investment of a Lifetime? The Long-term Labour Market Premiums Associated with a Postsecondary Education.* https://www150.statcan.gc.ca/n1/pub/11f0019m/11f0019m2014359-eng.htm

[4] Statistics Canada. (2019, October 18). *Student pathways through postsecondary education in Canada, 2010 to 2015.* The Daily. https://www150.statcan.gc.ca/n1/daily-quotidien/191018/dq191018a-eng.htm

[5] Ontario Colleges Application Service. (2022). *College Tuition Fees in Ontario.* https://www.ontariocolleges.ca/en/colleges/paying-for-college

[6] Usher, A. (2021). *The State of Postsecondary Education in Canada, 2021.* Toronto: Higher Education Strategy Associates. https://higheredstrategy.com/wp-content/uploads/2022/01/HESA_SPEC_2021.pdf

[7] Manson, M. (2022). *How to Get Motivated and Take Action.* Infinity Squared Media LLC. https://markmanson.net/how-to-get-motivated

[8] Dweck, C. (2007). *Mindset: The new psychology of success.* Random House Publishing.

[9] Ringel, M. (2013, September 30). *You Must Try, and then You Must Ask.* Ringel on Random – A Lab Notebook of Life. http://www.mattringel.com/2013/09/30/you-must-try-and-then-you-must-ask/

[10] Hadfield, C. (2013). *An astronaut's guide to life on earth.* RandomHouse of Canada.

[11] Harris, P. (2014, April 12). *How many jobs do Canadians hold in a lifetime?* Workopolis. https://careers.workopolis.com/advice/how-many-jobs-do-

canadians-hold-in-a-lifetime/

[12] Ontario Colleges Application Service. (2022). *Skilled Trades Programs and Careers in the Trades.*
https://www.ontariocolleges.ca/en/apply/skilled-trades

[13] Carnevale, A. P., Cheah, B., and Hanson, A. R. (2015). *The Economic Value of College Majors.* Georgetown University Center on Education and the Workforce. https://cew.georgetown.edu/wp-content/uploads/Exec-Summary-web-B.pdf

[14] Statistics Canada. (2019, November 5). *Student debt from all sources, by province of study and level of study.* DOI: https://doi.org/10.25318/3710003601-eng

[15] Astin, A. W. (1984). Student Involvement: A Development Theory for Higher Education. *Journal of College Student Development*, 40, 518-529.

[16] Ibid.

[17] Gorman, K., Bruns, C., Chin, C., Fitzpatrick, N., Koenig, L., LeViness, P., Sokolowski, K. (2021). *Annual Survey: 2021.* The Association for University and College Counseling Center Directors. https://www.aucccd.org/assets/2020-21%20Annual%20Survey%20Report%20Public%20Survey.pdf

[18] Linden, B., Boyes, R., & Stuart, H. (2021). Cross-sectional trend analysis of the NCHA II survey data on Canadian post-secondary student mental health and wellbeing from 2013 to 2019. *BMC public health*, 21(1), 590. DOI: https://doi.org/10.1186/s12889-021-10622-1

[19] Ratey, Dr. J. (2008). *Spark: The revolutionary new science of exercise and the brain.* Hachette Book Group, Inc.

[20] Coren, Dr. S. (1996). *Sleep thieves: An eye-opening exploration into the science and mysteries of sleep.* Free Press Paperbacks.

[21] Dr. Stanley Coren, as cited in Posen, D. (2016, March 8). *Sleep and Families.* The Vanier Institute of the Family. https://vanierinstitute.ca/sleep-families/#:~:text=Coren%20states%20that%20%E2%80%9Cone%20hour's,MRIs%20show%20the%20same%20thing.

[22] Breus, Dr. M. (2018, April 17). *Here's Why You Can't Think Straight When You're Sleep Deprived.* The Sleep Doctor. https://thesleepdoctor.com/2018/04/17/heres-why-you-cant-think-straight-when-youre-sleep-deprived/

[23] Statistics Canada. (2019, October). *Student pathways through postsecondary education in Canada, 2010 to 2015.* The Daily. https://www150.statcan.gc.ca/n1/daily-quotidien/191018/dq191018a-eng.htm

[24] Walsh, G. (2018). *The Cost of Credentials: The Shift Burden of Post-Secondary Tuition in Canada.* RBC. http://www.rbc.com/economics/economic-reports/pdf/other-reports/Tuition_June2018.pdf

[25] Ma, X. & Frempong, G. (2013). Profiles of Canadian Postsecondary Education Dropouts. *Alberta Journal of Educational Research*, 59(2), 141-161. https://eric.ed.gov/?id=EJ1028030

[26] Statistics Canada. (2019, October). *Student pathways through postsecondary education in Canada, 2010 to 2015.* The Daily. https://www150.statcan.gc.ca/n1/daily-quotidien/191018/dq191018a-eng.htm

www.ingramcontent.com/pod-product-compliance
Lightning Source LLC
Chambersburg PA
CBHW040312170426
43195CB00020B/2951